D1194836

FBC
3-
11/18

Printed in China

中国国家汉办赠送
Donated by Hanban, China

编 委 会

项目指导

许琳　王路江　曲德林

内容审定专家

赵金铭　姜明宝

总体设计

负责人：马箭飞　毛悦

宋继华　谭春健　梁彦民　赵雪梅

课文编写

主　编：马箭飞

副主编：毛悦

编　者：谭春健　梁彦民　赵雪梅　刘长征　陈若君　张媛媛　王轩　王枫

练习编写

负责人：陈军　赵秀娟

梁菲　李先银　杨慧真　魏耕耘　李泓

生词翻译

高明乐　张旭

故事、情景

张作民　卢岚岚

教学实验

负责人：迟兰英

毛悦　赵秀娟　陈军　魏耕耘　杨慧真　李泓　袁金春

文字审核

周婉梅

测试研发

负责人：谢小庆

彭恒利　鲁新民　姜德梧　任杰　张晋军　李慧　李桂梅

技术开发、技术支持

负责人：宋继华　许建红

北京长城汉语中心

北京语言大学电教中心

Hanban

中国国家汉办重点规划教材

GREAT WALL CHINESE

长城汉语

Essentials in Communication 生存交际 1

WORKBOOK

练习册

北京语言大学出版社
BEIJING LANGUAGE AND CULTURE UNIVERSITY PRESS

图书在版编目（CIP）数据

生存交际（1）练习册／马箭飞主编．－北京：北京
语言大学出版社，2010重印
（长城汉语）
ISBN 978-7-5619-1622-3

Ⅰ．生…　Ⅱ．马…　Ⅲ．汉语－对外汉语教学－习
题　Ⅳ．H195.4-44

中国版本图书馆CIP数据核字（2006）第034544号

书　　　名：长城汉语　生存交际练习册　一级
责任印制：汪学发

出版发行：北京语言大学出版社
社　　　址：北京市海淀区学院路15号　　　邮政编码：100083
网　　　址：www.blcup.com
电　　　话：发行部 82303648 / 3591 / 3651
　　　　　　编辑部 82303647
　　　　　　读者服务部 82303653 / 3908
　　　　　　网上订购电话 82303668
　　　　　　客户服务信箱 service@blcup.net
印　　　刷：北京联兴盛业印刷股份有限公司
经　　　销：全国新华书店

版　　　次：2006年4月第1版　　2010年8月第5次印刷
开　　　本：889毫米 x 1194毫米　1 / 16　　印张：10.75
字　　　数：185千字
书　　　号：ISBN 978-7-5619-1622-3/H·06075
　　　　　　03500

凡有印装质量问题，本社负责调换，电话：82303590

GREAT WALL CHINESE

前　言

本练习册与《长城汉语》"生存交际"课本相配套。

"长城汉语"以培养学习者的汉语交际能力为主要目标，运用网络、多媒体课件、面授、课本和练习册等多元学习方式，采用即时跟踪学习进度和测试学习效果的管理模式，依托丰富的教学资源，向学习者提供个性化的学习方案，以满足海内外汉语学习者任何时间、任何地点、任何水平的学习需求。

对应《长城汉语》"生存交际"课本每个单元的语音、汉字、词语、语法点、交际要点以及任务目标，同时本着由易到难、循序渐进的原则，本练习册的每个单元设计了语音练习、词汇练习、语法练习、交际练习和汉字练习。练习的设计目标明确，形式灵活多样，突出了语言的交际性和实用性，练习的内容突出了语言的基础知识和基本技能。为充分体现练习册的辅助作用，练习中不出现生词，以使学习者能够集中精力进行《长城汉语》主体内容的学习。完成本练习册，可以帮助学习者复习和巩固所学的语言知识，掌握学习内容，达到《长城汉语》"生存交际"的学习目标。

《长城汉语》课本以"创业"、"爱情"、"传奇"、"当代"四个故事为线索，话题涉及经济、文化、体育、伦理等领域，人物有来自不同国家的留学生麦克、玛丽、金太成、山口和子、菲雅以及他们的中国朋友张圆圆、赵玉兰、王杨、李冬生等。为了便于学生理解，增强趣味性，我们在练习册中沿用了课本故事中的人物和话题，并设计了部分看图练习。

编者

Preface

This workbook is an accompaniment of the textbook of *Great Wall Chinese: Essentials in Communication*.

The goal of *Great Wall Chinese* is to develop learners' Chinese communicative competence. Different means of teaching, such as on-line and multimedia coursewares, face-to-face teaching in class, textbooks and workbooks etc. are employed, and the management mode to monitor learners' progress and to test the learning effect is also used. Individualized learning plans with the backing of rich teaching resources are provided, so as to meet the needs of Chinese learning at any time, any place, and any level in China or overseas.

The courseware of *Great Wall Chinese* comprises two parts: the text and the exercises. And the exercises are divided into three sections: Communication Skills, Words and Expressions, and Grammar. This workbook is compiled to supplement on-line learning. Corresponding to the learning subject and goals of each unit in *Great Wall Chinese: Essentials in Communication*, we designed a variety of exercises in pronunciation, words and expressions, grammar, communication skills and Chinese characters in line with the principle of systematic and progressive learning. The exercises in this book feature a clear aim and varied forms with an emphasis on communication and practicality by focusing on basic language knowledge and skills. There is no new word in the exercises so that the learner can concentrate on the learning of the principal part of *Great Wall Chinese*. Doing the exercises will help the learner review and consolidate the language knowledge learned, thus achieving the goals set for *Great Wall Chinese: Essentials in Communication*.

Four stories run through the textbooks of *Great Wall Chinese*, which are Starting a Business, Love, a Legend, and the Contemporary Era. The topics cover economy, culture, sports, ethics, etc., by telling stories about several foreign students, Mike, Mary, Kim Tae-sung, Yamaguchi Kazuko, Faye, who came to China from different countries, and their Chinese friends, Zhang Yuanyuan, Zhao Yulan, Wang Yang, Li Dongsheng, etc. In order to facilitate the learners' understanding and make the learning more interesting, this workbook follows the topics and characters in the stories of the textbook, and some picture-based exercises are added.

Compilers

目录 【CONTENTS】

CONTENTS

Unit One

第一单元

你好，我是麦克
Nǐ hǎo, wǒ shì Màikè

Hello, I'm Mike

Key Points

Subject	Greetings
Goals	Learn the basic ways to greet people, and tell one's own name and other's name
Grammar Points	• The personal pronouns "你，我，他／她，您，你们" • Questions with the interrogative pronoun "谁" • The "是" sentences：introduction and illustration

Focal Sentences	Major points in communication	Examples
	Frequently used greetings	你好！
	Polite greetings	您好！
	Introducing oneself	我是张芳芳。
	Identifying someone	他是谁？
	Introducing or identifying someone	他是李老师。

Words	你 好 我 是 您 你们 她 谁 他 老师 刘少华 赵玉兰 麦克 张芳芳 张圆圆 金太成 山口和子 王杨 玛丽 菲雅 李冬生 陈晓红
Chinese Characters	我 是 你 好 您 们 她 谁 他 老 师
Phonetics	Syllable initials: n h Syllable finals: a o e i Tones: 1 2 3 4

Exercises

Ⅰ. Pronunciation

1 Read the following *Pinyin* aloud and pay attention to their different pronunciations.

nǐ	——	lǐ	nà	——	là
lǎo	——	nǎo	náo	——	ráo
hā	——	fā	hóng	——	fāng
wǒ	——	wǎ	bā	——	bō
tā	——	tè	zhào	——	shào
hé	——	hǎo	wáng	——	yáng

2 Read the following *Pinyin* aloud and pay attention to their different tones.

nā	ná	nǎ	nà
hāo	háo	hǎo	hào
tā	nín	wǒ	shì
fāng	wáng	lǎo	lì

3 Read the following words aloud.

我们	他们	老师	你好
wǒmen	tāmen	lǎoshī	nǐ hǎo

Ⅱ.Words and Expressions

1 Match the correct pronoun to its corresponding picture.
(Which pronoun are the people in the pictures likely to use?)

①

A 我 wǒ

②

B 你 nǐ

③

C 他 tā

④

D 她 tā

⑤

E 你们 nǐmen

2 Pick out the word that does not belong to the group.

① 你　　　我　　　她　　　你们　　　　　（　　　）
　　nǐ　　　wǒ　　　tā　　　nǐmen

② 你　　　是　　　我　　　他　　　　　　（　　　）
　　nǐ　　　shì　　　wǒ　　　tā

③ 谁　　　她　　　他　　　我　　　　　　（　　　）
　　shuí　　tā　　　tā　　　wǒ

④ 麦克　　王杨　　　老师　　　玛丽　　　（　　　）
　　Màikè　Wáng Yáng　lǎoshī　Mǎlì

⑤ 我　　　你　　　她　　　您　　　　　　（　　　）
　　wǒ　　　nǐ　　　tā　　　nín

3 Choose the right word to fill in the blank.

是	好	谁	你们	老师
shì	hǎo	shuí	nǐmen	lǎoshī

① 他 是_____?
　Tā shì

② 你_____！我 是 玛丽。
　Nǐ　　　　Wǒ shì Mǎlì.

③ 他 是 李_____。
　Tā shì Lǐ

④ 我_____金 太成。
　Wǒ　　　Jīn Tàichéng.

⑤ _____好！我 是 麦克。
　　　　hǎo!　Wǒ shì Màikè.

Ⅲ. Grammar

Grammar Points

● The personal pronouns "你", "我", "他／她", "您" and "你们"

你　好!
Nǐ　hǎo!

我　是　菲雅。
Wǒ　shì　Fēiyǎ.

他／她　是　老师。
Tā／Tā　shì　lǎoshī.

您　好!
Nín　hǎo!

你们　　好!
Nǐmen　hǎo!

● Questions with the interrogative pronoun "谁"

Personal pronoun＋是＋谁?

她　是　谁?
Tā　shì　shuí?

你　是　谁?
Nǐ　shì　shuí?

● The "是" sentences

Personal pronoun+ 是 +noun

我　　是　　　山口　和子。
Wǒ　　shì　　Shānkǒu Hézǐ.

他　　是　　　老师。
Tā　　shì　　lǎoshī.

---

1 Choose the right word to fill in the blank.

① _____好!　我 是　玛丽。　　　　（她　　你）
　　hǎo!　Wǒ shì　Mǎlì.　　　　　　　　tā　　nǐ

② _____是　麦克。　　　　　　　　（她　　他）
　　shì　Màikè.　　　　　　　　　　　　tā　　tā

③ 老师，_____好!　　　　　　　　（您　　你）
　　Lǎoshī　　　　hǎo!　　　　　　　　　nín　　nǐ

④ 他 是_____?　　　　　　　　　　（好　　谁）
　　Tā shì　　　　　　　　　　　　　　　hǎo　shuí

⑤ 你们　好!　我_____玛丽。　　　（是　　好）
　　Nǐmen hǎo! Wǒ　　　　　Mǎlì.　　　　shì　　hǎo

2 Complete the following dialogues.

① A：你 是_____?
　　　Nǐ shì

　 B：我 是　麦克。
　　　Wǒ shì　Màikè.

② A: ＿＿＿＿＿＿＿＿＿＿是 谁？
　　　　　　　　　　　　shì shuí?

B: 他 是 金 太成。
　　Tā shì Jīn Tàichéng.

③ A: 你们 好！ 我＿＿＿＿＿＿＿＿＿李 冬生。
　　　Nǐmen hǎo! Wǒ　　　　　　　　　Lǐ Dōngshēng.

B: 您 好！
　　Nín hǎo!

④ A: 我＿＿＿＿＿＿＿赵 玉兰， 他＿＿＿＿＿＿刘 少华。
　　　Wǒ　　　　　　Zhào Yùlán, tā　　　　Liú Shàohuá.

B: 你们 好！
　　Nǐmen hǎo!

⑤ A: ＿＿＿＿＿＿＿＿＿＿＿＿＿＿＿＿＿？

B: 她 是 张 圆圆。
　　Tā shì Zhāng Yuányuan.

IV. Communication Skills

1 Match the sentences in the two columns to form a conversation.

① 你们 好！ 我 是李 冬生。　　A 她 是 　王 　杨。
　Nǐmen hǎo! Wǒ shì Lǐ Dōngshēng.　　Tā shì Wáng Yáng.

② 他 是 谁?　　　　　　　　　B 您 　好! 老师。
　Tā shì shuí?　　　　　　　　　Nín hǎo! Lǎoshī.

③ 你 好! 玛丽。　　　　　　　C 我 是 张 　圆圆。
　Nǐ hǎo! Mǎlì.　　　　　　　　Wǒ shì Zhāng Yuányuan.

④ 她 是 谁?　　　　　　　　　D 你 　好! 菲雅。
　Tā shì shuí?　　　　　　　　　Nǐ hǎo! Fēiyǎ.

⑤ 你 是 谁?　　　　　　　　　E 他 是 金 太成。
　Nǐ shì shuí?　　　　　　　　　Tā shì Jīn Tàichéng.

2 Complete the following dialogues.

① A: 您 好! 我 是_____。
　　Nín hǎo! Wǒ shì

　B: _____! 我 是 李 冬生。
　　　　　　　　　　Wǒ shì Lǐ Dōngshēng.

　A: _____?

　B: 他 是 金 太成。
　　Tā shì Jīn Tàichéng.

　A: 她 是 谁?
　　Tā shì shuí?

　B: _____是 王 杨。
　　　　　　　shì Wáng Yáng.

② A: 你 好！我 是＿＿＿＿＿＿＿＿＿＿＿。
　　 Nǐ hǎo! Wǒ shì

　　B: 你 好！我 是＿＿＿＿＿＿＿＿＿＿＿。
　　 Nǐ hǎo! Wǒ shì

　　A: 他 是＿＿＿＿＿＿＿＿＿？
　　 Tā shì

　　B: ＿＿＿＿＿＿＿＿＿＿＿＿＿。

　　C: (To A, B) ＿＿＿＿好！
　　　　　　　　　　hǎo!

V. Chinese Characters

Basic Knowledge

- ● Basic strokes of Chinese characters (1)

Stroke	Name of the stroke	Way of writing the strokes	Examples
一	(héng) Horizontal stroke	From left to right	一　二　三
丨	(shù) Vertical stroke	From top to bottom	十　干　丰

● Characteristics of the shape of the Chinese character

Chinese characters are square-shaped. No matter how many strokes one character has, it should be written in a square space. For example,

● The composition of Chinese characters

Chinese characters are composed of some basic components, to which you have to pay attention when you learn to read and write them. It will be helpful to improve your learning efficiency.

好 —— 女+子
她 —— 女+也

1 Practise writing the strokes.

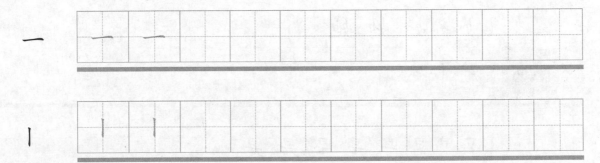

2 Compose the following radicals into characters and form words with them.

亻 尔 　　 (　　) _____

亻 也 　　 (　　) _____

亻 门 　　 (　　) _____

3 Practise writing the characters.

丿 二 于 手 我 我 我

| 我 | 我 | 我 | | | | | | | | |

丿 亻 亻 亻 亻 你 你 你

| 你 | 你 | 你 | | | | | | | | |

丿 亻 亻 他 他

| 他 | 他 | 他 | | | | | | | | |

乛 女 女 如 如 她

| 她 | 她 | 她 | | | | | | | | |

丶 丨 冂 日 旦 早 旱 昰 是

| 是 | 是 | 是 | | | | | | | | |

乛 女 女 女 好 好

| 好 | 好 | 好 | | | | | | | | |

Unit Two

第二单元

我姓金，叫金　太成

Wǒ xìng Jīn,　jiào　Jīn　Tàichéng

My surname is Kim, and my full name is Kim Tae-sung

Key Points

Subject	Family names, given names
Goals	Learn to ask and tell family names and given names
Grammar Points	• Special questions with "什么" • The yes-or-no questions • The adverb "也"

Focal Sentences	Major points in communication	Examples
	Basic ways to ask and tell names	您贵姓? 你叫什么名字? ——我姓金，我叫金太成。
	Beginning introducing someone	我来介绍一下儿。
	Expressing apologies	对不起。
	Responding to apologies	没关系。
	Greetings on first meeting	认识您很高兴。

Words and Phrases	姓 叫 什么 名字 对不起 没关系 嗯 学生 吗 贵姓 请问（请、问） 认识 很 高兴 也 来 介绍 一下儿
Chinese Characters	姓 叫 什 么 名 字 对 不 起 没 关 系 嗯 学 生 吗 贵 请 问 认 识 很 高 兴 也 来 介 绍 一 下 儿
Phonetics	Syllable initials: b p m Syllable finals: ai ao ei en Tones: 1 2 3 4

Exercises

 Ⅰ.Pronunciation

1 Read the following *Pinyin* aloud and pay attention to their different pronunciations.

míng — níng	mài — nài
duì — tuì	dài — tài
hěn — fěn	lái — nǎi
yī — yě	dà — tè
lái — léi	mǎi — měi
hēi — hěn	mèi — mèn

2 Read the following *Pinyin* aloud and pay attention to their different tones.

yē	yé	yě	yè
tā	méi	mǎi	mài
mā	yáng	qǐng	wèn
shénme	míngzi	xuésheng	rènshi

3 Read the following words aloud.

什么	名字	对不起	没关系	学生
shénme	míngzi	duìbuqǐ	méi guānxi	xuésheng

请问	贵姓	认识	高兴	介绍
qǐng wèn	guìxìng	rènshi	gāoxìng	jièshào

II.Words and Expressions

1 Pick out the word that does not belong to the group.

① 介绍　　问　　什么　　认识　　　　　　　（　　　）
jièshào　wèn　shénme　rènshi

② 也　　请　　来　　是　　　　　　　　　　（　　　）
yě　qǐng　lái　shì

③ 名字　　学生　　老师　　介绍　　　　　　　（　　　）
míngzi　xuésheng　lǎoshī　jièshào

④ 叫　　很　　问　　姓　　　　　　　　　　（　　　）
jiào　hěn　wèn　xìng

⑤ 也　　很　　吗　　　　　　　　　　　　　（　　　）
yě　hěn　ma

2 Choose the right word to fill in the blank (1).

认识　　也　　很　　来　　姓
rènshi　yě　hěn　lái　xìng

① 请　　问，　您　贵_____?
Qǐng　wèn,　nín　guì

② 他_____是　老师。
Tā　　　　shì　lǎoshī.

③ 她_____山口　和子。
　 Tā　　　　　Shānkǒu Hézǐ.

④ 请　你_____介绍　　一下儿。
　 Qǐng nǐ　　　　　jièshào　yíxiàr.

⑤ 张　　芳芳　_____高兴。
　 Zhāng Fāngfāng　　　　gāoxìng.

Choose the right word to fill in the blank (2).

叫	高兴	什么	介绍	学生
jiào	gāoxìng	shénme	jièshào	xuésheng

① 我　来_____一下儿，我　姓　　王　，我　叫　王　　杨。
　 Wǒ lái　　　　　yíxiàr,　wǒ xìng Wáng, wǒ jiào Wáng Yáng.

② 你_____张　　　圆圆　　吗?
　 Nǐ　　　　　Zhāng Yuányuan　ma?

③ 请　　问，　你 姓_____?
　 Qǐng　wèn,　nǐ xìng

④ 认识　　您 我 也　很_____。
　 Rènshi　nín wǒ yě hěn

⑤ 张　　芳芳　　是_____吗?
　 Zhāng Fāngfāng　shì　　　　　ma?

III. Grammar

Grammar Points

● Special questions with "什么"

Subject ＋ Verb ＋ 什么 ＋ Noun?

他　姓　　什么?
Tā　xìng　　shénme?

你　叫　　什么　　名字?
Nǐ　jiào　　shénme　　míngzi?

● The yes-or-no questions

Subject ＋ Adverb ＋ Verb ＋ Noun / Pronoun ＋ 吗?

他　是　老师　　吗?
Tā　shì　lǎoshī　　ma?

你　也　认识　　麦克／他　　吗?
Nǐ　yě　rènshi　　Màikè／tā　　ma?

● The adverb "也"

Subject ＋ 也 ＋ Verb ＋ Noun

他　也　是　　学生。
Tā　yě　shì　xuésheng.

我 也 认识 张 老师。
Wǒ yě rènshi Zhāng lǎoshī.

Subject + 也 + Adverb + Adjective

我 也 很 高兴。
Wǒ yě hěn gāoxìng.

1 Determine if the following sentences are right or wrong and correct the wrong one(s).

① 请 问, 您 贵姓 什么?   (   )
Qǐng wèn, nín guìxìng shénme?

_____

② 你 叫 什么 名字 吗?   (   )
Nǐ jiào shénme míngzi ma?

_____

③ 她 也 认识 李 老师, 我 认识 李 老师。   (   )
Tā yě rènshi Lǐ lǎoshī, wǒ rènshi Lǐ lǎoshī.

_____

④ 玛丽 是 也 学生。   (   )
Mǎlì shì yě xuésheng.

_____

⑤ 他 是 老师 什么?   (   )
Tā shì lǎoshī shénme?

_____

2 Complete the following dialogues.

① A: 你 是＿＿＿＿＿＿＿＿＿＿＿＿＿＿＿？
　　 Nǐ shì

　 B: 是， 我 是 老师。
　　 Shì, wǒ shì lǎoshī.

② A: 你＿＿＿＿＿＿＿＿＿＿＿＿＿＿＿＿？
　　 Nǐ

　 B: 我 姓 李。
　　 Wǒ xìng Lǐ.

③ A: 她＿＿＿＿＿＿＿＿＿＿＿＿＿＿＿？
　　 Tā

　 B: 她 叫 山口 和子。
　　 Tā jiào Shānkǒu Hézǐ.

④ A: 认识 你 很 高兴。
　　 Rènshi nǐ hěn gāoxìng.

　 B: 认识 你＿＿＿＿＿＿＿＿＿＿。
　　 Rènshi nǐ

⑤ A: 我 姓 张。
　　 Wǒ xìng Zhāng.

　 B: 我 也＿＿＿＿＿＿＿＿＿＿＿。
　　 Wǒ yě

IV. Communication Skills

1 Choose the correct response.

① A: 您　贵姓？
　　 Nín　guìxìng?

　　 B: _____

　　 ⓐ 我　姓　金。　　　　ⓑ 我　叫　金　太成。
　　　　 Wǒ　xìng　Jīn.　　　　 Wǒ　jiào　Jīn Tàichéng.

② A: 对不起。
　　 Duìbuqǐ.

　　 B: _____

　　 ⓐ 谢谢！ Xièxie!　　　　ⓑ 没关系。Méi guānxi.

③ A: 认识　你很　高兴。
　　 Rènshi　nǐ hěn gāoxìng.

　　 B: _____

　　 ⓐ 我　也很　高兴。　　ⓑ 我　也不　认识你。
　　　　 Wǒ　yě hěn　gāoxìng.　　 Wǒ　yě　bú　rènshi nǐ.

④ A: 你　叫　什么　名字？
　　 Nǐ　jiào　shénme　míngzi?

　　 B: _____

　　 ⓐ 我　姓　王。　　　　ⓑ 我　叫　王杨。
　　　　 Wǒ　xìng　Wáng.　　　　 Wǒ　jiào Wáng Yáng.

⑤　A: 你　认识　她　吗?

　　　　Nǐ　rènshi　tā　ma?

　　B: _____

　　　[a] 他　是　李　老师。　　　[b] 他　不　是　王　老师。

　　　　　Tā　shì　Lǐ　lǎoshī.　　　　Tā　bú　shì　Wáng lǎoshī.

2 Complete the following dialogues.

A: _____。

B: 没　关系。

　　Méi　guānxi.

A: _____?

B: 我　是　学生。

　　Wǒ　shì　xuésheng.

A: _____?

B: 我　叫　玛丽。

　　Wǒ　jiào　Mǎlì.

A: 我　是　麦克, _____。

　　Wǒ　shì　Màikè,

B: 认识　你　我　也　很　高兴。

　　Rènshi　nǐ　wǒ　yě　hěn　gāoxìng.

A: 我 来＿＿＿＿＿＿＿，她 姓 王， 叫＿＿＿＿＿＿＿。
   Wǒ lái   tā xìng Wáng, jiào

B: 你 好！我 姓 山口， 叫 山口 和子。
   Nǐ hǎo! Wǒ xìng Shānkǒu, jiào Shānkǒu Hézǐ.

C: 你 好！你＿＿＿＿＿＿＿？
   Nǐ hǎo! Nǐ

B: 我 也 是 学生。
   Wǒ yě shì xuésheng.

C: ＿＿＿＿＿＿＿＿＿＿＿＿＿＿＿＿＿。

B: ＿＿＿＿＿＿＿＿＿＿＿＿＿＿＿＿＿。

Ⅴ. Chinese Characters

Basic Knowledge

● Basic strokes of Chinese characters (2)

Stroke	Name of the stroke	Way of writing the stroke	Examples
丿	(piě) Left-falling stroke	From the right-top to the left-bottom	八 千
乀	(nà) Right-falling stroke	From the left-top to the right-bottom	八 大

● Basic components of Chinese characters

亻 The radical single 亻 (dān rén páng). The character 人 is originally developed from the image of a man. When it is taken as a component to form a character it is written as 亻. The original meanings of the characters with 亻 as their radical are generally related to "man". For example, 你(nǐ), 他(tā), 们(men).

女 The radical 女(nǚ zì páng). The character 女 is originally developed from the image of a woman. The original meanings of the characters with 女 as their radical are generally related to "woman". For example，妈(mā), 姐(jiě), 妹(mèi), 她(tā).

1 Practise writing the strokes.

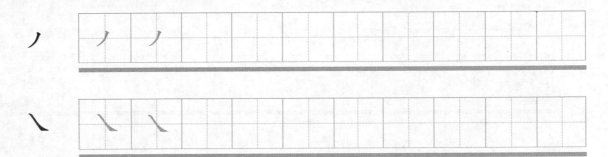

2 Compose the following radicals into characters and form words with them.

3 Practise writing the characters.

一 丁 イ 不

不 | 不 | 不 | | | | | | | | | | |

ノ イ 仁 什

什 | 什 | 什 | | | | | | | | | | |

ノ 厶 么

么 | 么 | 么 | | | | | | | | | | |

ノ ク ク タ 夕 名 名

名 | 名 | 名 | | | | | | | | | | |

丶 丷 宀 宀 宁 字

字 | 字 | 字 | | | | | | | | | | |

フ ヌ ヌ 对 对

对 | 对 | 对 | | | | | | | | | | |

ノ 亻 ニ 牛 生

生	生	生										

し 女 女 女 如 如 姓 姓

姓	姓	姓										

丶 亻 门 门 问 问

问	问	问										

丶 讠 认 认

认	认	认										

丶 讠 讠 识 识 识 识

识	识	识										

ノ ノ 彳 彳 彳 彳 彳 很 很

很	很	很										

丶 亠 古 古 古 高 高 高 高

高	高	高										

丶 ⺍ ⺌ 兴 兴

兴	兴	兴											

⼁ ⺄ 也

也	也	也											

一 ⼂ ⼮ 平 平 来 来

来	来	来											

Unit Three

第三单元

我　从　英国　伦敦　来
Wǒ　cóng　Yīngguó　Lúndūn　lái

I come from London of the Great Britain

Key Points

Subject	Nationality and place of one's origin	
Goals	Learn to ask and tell one's nationality and origin	
Grammar Points	• Using "不" to express negation • Special questions with "哪儿" or "什么地方" • The questions with "……吧"	
Focal Sentences	Major points in communication	Examples
	Basic ways to ask and tell one's nationality	你是哪国人？ ——我是日本人。
	Basic ways to ask and tell one's origin	您是哪儿人？ ——我是北京人。 你是日本什么地方人？ ——我是日本东京人。
	Polite ways to ask questions	请问，您是哪国人？
	Polite ways to make a request	请再说一遍。
	Expressing thanks	谢谢！
	Telling where one is from	我从英国伦敦来。
Words and Phrases	从 来 姓名 国籍 再 说 一 遍 哪 国 人 哦 的 护照 给 谢谢 吧 不 爸爸 妈妈 地方 但 英国 伦敦 罗森 法国 美国 日本 韩国 北京 上海 广东 东京 中国	
Chinese Characters	国 籍 再 说 遍 哪 人 哦 的 护 照 给 谢 吧 不 爸 妈 从 地 方 但 北 京 中	
Phonetics	Syllable initials: b p m Syllable finals: ai ao ei en Tones: 1 2 3 4	

Exercises

Ⅰ. Pronunciation

1 Read the following *Pinyin* aloud and pay attention to their different pronunciations.

bà	—	pà	biàn	—	piàn
nǎ	—	mǎ	míng	—	níng
hù	—	fù	dōng	—	tōng
ài	—	àn	dài	—	dàn
běi	—	běn	xiè	—	xià
hǎi	—	hǎn	lái	—	láo

2 Read the following *Pinyin* aloud and pay attention to their different tones.

bā	bá	bǎ	bà
hū	hú	hǔ	hù
fēi	guó	fǎ	biàn
yì tiān	yì nián	yì kǒu	yí gè

3 Read the following words aloud.

姓名	护照	中国	北京
xìngmíng	hùzhào	Zhōngguó	Běijīng

爸爸	妈妈	谢谢	地方
bàba	māma	xièxie	dìfang

Ⅱ.Words and Expressions

1 Pick out the word that does not belong to the group.

① 爸爸   妈妈   老师   护照   (   )
   bàba   māma   lǎoshī   hùzhào

② 从   再   也   很   (   )
   cóng   zài   yě   hěn

③ 姓名   谢谢   国籍   地方   (   )
   xìngmíng   xièxie   guójí   dìfang

④ 叫   给   说   但   (   )
   jiào   gěi   shuō   dàn

⑤ 美国   法国   北京   日本   (   )
   Měiguó   Fǎguó   Běijīng   Rìběn

2 Choose the right word to fill in the blank (1).

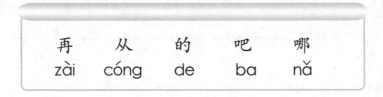

再	从	的	吧	哪
zài	cóng	de	ba	nǎ

① 你_____哪儿 来?
   Nǐ   nǎr   lái?

② 他 是_____国 人?
   Tā shì   guó rén?

③ 你　是　英国　人＿＿＿＿＿＿？
　Nǐ　shì　Yīngguó　rén

④ 请　＿＿＿＿＿＿　说　一　遍。
　Qǐng　　　　　shuō　yí　biàn.

⑤ 您　是　玛丽＿＿＿＿＿＿妈妈　吧？认识　您　很　高兴。
　Nín　shì　Mǎlì　　　　māma　ba? Rènshi nín hěn gāoxìng.

Choose the right word to fill in the blank (2).

说	但	给	地方	姓名
shuō	dàn	gěi	dìfang	xìngmíng

① 对不起，　请　您　再＿＿＿＿＿一　遍。
　Duìbuqǐ,　qǐng　nín　zài　　　　yí　biàn.

② 请　问，您　的＿＿＿＿＿＿？
　Qǐng　wèn, nín　de

③ 我　的　护照。＿＿＿＿＿＿你。
　Wǒ　de　hùzhào.　　　nǐ.

④ 我　爸爸　是　美国人，＿＿＿＿＿我　妈妈　是　英国　人。
　Wǒ　bàba shì Měiguó rén,　　　wǒ māma shì　Yīngguó　rén.

⑤ 你　是　中国　什么＿＿＿＿＿人？
　Nǐ　shì　Zhōngguó　shénme　　　rén?

III. Grammar

Grammar Points

- Using "不" to express negation

  Subject + 不 + Verb + Noun/Pronoun

  李　冬生　　不　是　　学生。
  Lǐ Dōngshēng bú shì xuésheng.

  我　不　认识　她。
  Wǒ bú rènshi tā.

- Special questions with "哪儿" or "什么地方"

  Subject + Verb + 哪儿／什么地方 +Noun

  玛丽　是　哪儿／什么　地方　人？
  Mǎlì shì nǎr / shénme dìfang rén?

  Subject + Preposition + 哪儿／什么地方 + Verb

  你　从　哪儿／什么　地方　来？
  Nǐ cóng nǎr / shénme dìfang lái?

- The questions with "……吧"

  Subject + Verb + Noun+ 吧？

  他　是　你的　老师　吧？
  Tā shì nǐ de lǎoshī ba?

  你　是　日本　人　吧？
  Nǐ shì Rìběn rén ba?

1 Transform the following sentences into their negative form, using "不".

① 他 是 韩国 人。
Tā shì Hánguó rén.

→ _____

② 她 姓 张。
Tā xìng Zhāng.

→ _____

③ 他 是 我 的 老师。
Tā shì wǒ de lǎoshī.

→ _____

④ 张 圆圆 很 高兴。
Zhāng Yuányuan hěn gāoxìng.

→ _____

⑤ 我 也 认识 李 老师。
Wǒ yě rènshi Lǐ lǎoshī.

→ _____

2 Transform the following sentences into interrogative sentences according to the instructions.

① 我 姓 李。
Wǒ xìng Lǐ.

→ _____ (什么 shénme)

② 我 是 日本 人。
Wǒ shì Rìběn rén.

→ _____ (哪 nǎ)

③ 我　　从　　　上海　　　来。
　　Wǒ　cóng　Shànghǎi　lái.

　　→＿＿＿＿＿＿＿＿＿＿＿＿＿＿＿＿＿＿＿＿（哪儿　nǎr）

④ 玛丽　　是　　　英国　　伦敦　　人。
　　Mǎlì　shì　Yīngguó　Lúndūn　rén.

　　→＿＿＿＿＿＿＿＿＿＿＿＿＿＿＿（什么地方　shénme dìfang）

⑤ 他　　是　　　老师。
　　Tā　shì　　lǎoshī.

　　→＿＿＿＿＿＿＿＿＿＿＿＿＿＿＿＿＿＿＿＿（吧　ba）

3 Complete the following dialogues.

① A: 你　是＿＿＿＿＿＿＿＿＿＿？
　　　Nǐ　shì

　 B: 我　是　　英国　　人。
　　　Wǒ　shì　Yīngguó　rén.

② A: 你　是　　英国＿＿＿＿＿＿＿＿人？
　　　Nǐ　shì　Yīngguó　　　　　rén?

　 B: 我　　是　英国　　伦敦　　人。
　　　Wǒ　shì　Yīngguó　Lúndūn　rén.

③ A: 他　从＿＿＿＿＿＿＿＿来?
　　　Tā　cóng　　　　　　lái?

　 B: 他　从　　广东　　来。
　　　Tā　cóng　Guǎngdōng　lái.

④ A: 你　爸爸　是　北京　人　吧?
　　　Nǐ　bàba　shì　Běijīng　rén　ba?

B: _____。

⑤ A: 你 是_____吗?
    Nǐ shì   ma?

B: 不，我 是 法国 人。
    Bù, wǒ shì Fǎguó rén.

Ⅳ. Communication Skills

1 Match the sentences in the two columns to form a conversation.

① 请 问，你 是 哪 国 人?
   Qǐng wèn, nǐ shì nǎ guó rén?

② 你 从 哪儿 来?
   Nǐ cóng nǎr lái?

③ 你 是 什么 地方 人?
   Nǐ shì shénme dìfang rén?

④ 你 的 护照?
   Nǐ de hùzhào?

⑤ 你 妈妈 是 哪儿 人?
   Nǐ māma shì nǎr rén?

A 我 妈妈 是
  Wǒ māma shì

上海 人。
Shànghǎi rén.

B 什么? 请 您
  Shénme? Qǐng nín

再 说 一 遍。
zài shuō yí biàn.

C 我 从 伦敦 来。
  Wǒ cóng Lúndūn lái.

D 我 是 美国 人。
  Wǒ shì Měiguó rén.

E 我 是 日本
  Wǒ shì Rìběn

东京 人。
Dōngjīng rén.

2 Complete the following dialogues.

① A: 你 好! 我 叫 麦克。
　　 Nǐ hǎo! Wǒ jiào Màikè.

　 B: _____! 我 叫 玛丽。
　　　　　　　　　　　 Wǒ jiào Mǎlì.

　 A: _____?

　 B: 我 从 英国 伦敦 来。_____?
　　　 Wǒ cóng Yīngguó Lúndūn lái.

　 A: 我 是 美国 人。
　　　 Wǒ shì Měiguó rén.

　 B: 认识 你 很 高兴。
　　　 Rènshi nǐ hěn gāoxìng.

　 A: _____。

　 B: 他 也 是 学生 吗?
　　　 Tā yě shì xuésheng ma?

　 A: _____, 他 是 老师。
　　　　　　　　　　　　 tā shì lǎoshī.

② A: 你 是 韩国 人 吧?
　　　 Nǐ shì Hánguó rén ba?

　 B: 什么? 请_____。
　　　 Shénme? Qǐng

　 A: 你 是 韩国 人 吗?
　　　 Nǐ shì Hánguó rén ma?

　 B: 不, _____, 我 是_____。
　　　 Bù, 　　　　　　　　　 wǒ shì

A: _____?

B: 我　是　日本　　东京　　人。_____?
　　Wǒ　shì　Rìběn　Dōngjīng　rén.

A: 我　是　北京　人。
　　Wǒ　shì　Běijīng　rén.

B: 你　爸爸、妈妈　也　是　北京　人　吗?
　　Nǐ　bàba、māma　yě　shì　Běijīng　rén　ma?

A: 我　爸爸　是　北京　人，但_____。
　　Wǒ　bàba　shì　Běijīng　rén, dàn

Ⅴ. Chinese Characters

Basic Knowledge

● Basic strokes of Chinese characters (3)

Stroke	Name of the stroke	Way of writing the stroke	Examples
丶	(diǎn) Dot	From the left-top to the right-bottom	兴　问
ノ	(tí) Rising stroke	From the left-bottom to the right-top	地　护

● Basic components of Chinese characters

讠   The radical 讠 (yán zì páng). The original meanings of the characters with 讠 as their radical are generally related to "speaking". For example, 请 (qǐng), 说 (shuō), 认 (rèn), 识 (shí), 谁 (shuí), 谢 (xiè).

口   The radical 口 (kǒu zì páng). It is originally developed from the image of the mouth of a man. The original meanings of the characters with 口 as their radical are generally related to "mouth". For example, 叫 (jiào), 吗 (ma), 吧 (ba), 哪 (nǎ).

1 Practise writing the strokes.

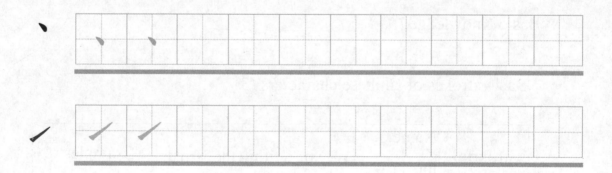

2 Compose the following radicals into characters and form words with them.

① 讠 人 (   ) _____

讠 只 (   ) _____

讠 青 (   ) _____

讠　兑　（　　）＿＿＿＿＿＿

讠　隹　（　　）＿＿＿＿＿＿

讠　射　（　　）＿＿＿＿＿＿

② 口　丩　（　　）＿＿＿＿＿＿

口　马　（　　）＿＿＿＿＿＿

口　巴　（　　）＿＿＿＿＿＿

口　那　（　　）＿＿＿＿＿＿

3　Practise writing the characters.

丿人

人	人	人										

丨口口中

中	中	中										

丨冂冂冃冃国国国

国	国	国										

丶 讠 讠 讠 讠 讠 讠 讠 说

说	说	说											

丿 亻 亻 白 白 的 的 的

的	的	的											

丨 冂 冂 叮 叩 叭 吧

吧	吧	吧											

丶 八 父 父 爷 爷 爸

爸	爸	爸											

乚 女 女 奵 妈 妈

妈	妈	妈											

丿 人 从 从

从	从	从											

一 十 土 圹 地 地

地	地	地											

丶一宁方

| 方 | 方 | 方 | | | | | | | | | | | | |

ノイ个们但但但

| 但 | 但 | 但 | | | | | | | | | | | | |

丨十才北北

| 北 | 北 | 北 | | | | | | | | | | | | |

丶一六市古亨京京

| 京 | 京 | 京 | | | | | | | | | | | | |

Unit Four

第四单元

我 在 一 家 公司　工作
Wǒ zài yì jiā gōngsī gōngzuò

I work in a company

Key Points

Subject	Occupations	
Goals	Learn to ask and tell one's occupation	
Grammar Points	<ul><li>Adverbials of time</li><li>Noun/pronoun + "的" + noun</li><li>Adverbials of place</li><li>The quantifier "个, 名, 家"</li></ul>	
Focal Sentences	**Major points in communication**	**Examples**
	Basic ways to ask and answer questions about someone's occupation	你做什么工作? ——我是教练。
	Asking and telling where someone works	你在哪儿工作? ——我在一家公司工作。
	Expressing one's likings	我喜欢这个工作。 我喜欢画画儿。
	Affirm/negate the other's questions or comments	对，我也工作。 不，我每天下午工作。
Words and Phrases	大家 教练 护士 名 大学生 家 公司 工作 秘书 好 每天 图书馆 下午 在 哪儿 部门经理 做 职员 记者 喜欢 这个 现在 画 画儿 啊 个 画家 珍妮 澳大利亚 东北 德国	
Chinese Characters	大 家 教 练 护 士 公 司 工 作 秘 书 每 天 图 书 馆 午 在 部 门 经 理 做 职 员 记 者 喜 欢 这 个 现 画 啊	
Phonetics	Syllable initials: d t f Syllable finals: u an ie uo Tones: half-third tone	

Exercises

Ⅰ. Pronunciation

1 Read the following *Pinyin* aloud and pay attention to their different pronunciations.

dà —— tà		tú —— dú	
bù —— pù		lǐ —— nǐ	
jiā —— qiā		jiào —— qiào	
jiā —— jiē		jià —— jiào	
wā —— wān		huà —— huàn	
liàn —— liàng		liàn —— luàn	

2 Read the following *Pinyin* aloud and pay attention to their different tones.

dā	dá	dǎ	dà
tiān	tián	diǎn	diàn
jiā	xué	hǎo	hù
shū	yuán	xǐ	bù

3 Read the following words aloud.

教练	护士	秘书	经理	记者	大学生
jiàoliàn	hùshi	mìshū	jīnglǐ	jìzhě	dàxuéshēng

大家	现在	喜欢	工作	公司	图书馆
dàjiā	xiànzài	xǐhuan	gōngzuò	gōngsī	túshūguǎn

Ⅱ.Words and Expressions

1 Pick out the word that does not belong to the group.

① 经理　　秘书　　公司　　职员　　　　（　　　）
　　jīnglǐ　　mìshū　　gōngsī　　zhíyuán

② 记者　　工作　　教练　　护士　　　　（　　　）
　　jìzhě　　gōngzuò　　jiàoliàn　　hùshi

③ 喜欢　　画家　　部门　　图书馆　　　（　　　）
　　xǐhuan　　huàjiā　　bùmén　　túshūguǎn

④ 名　　在　　个　　家　　　　　　　（　　　）
　　míng　　zài　　gè　　jiā

⑤ 每天　　大家　　现在　　下午　　　　（　　　）
　　měi tiān　dàjiā　xiànzài　　xiàwǔ

2 Choose the right word to fill in the blank (1).

做	在	家	画	名
zuò	zài	jiā	huà	míng

① 你＿＿＿＿＿＿＿＿＿哪儿　工作?
　　Nǐ　　　　　　　　　nǎr　gōngzuò?

② 玛丽　喜欢＿＿＿＿＿＿＿＿画儿。
　　Mǎlì　xǐhuan　　　　　　huàr.

③ 他 是 一＿＿＿＿＿＿＿＿＿大学生。
　　Tā shì yì　　　　　　　　dàxuéshēng.

④ 李 冬生 ＿＿＿＿＿＿＿＿什么　工作?
　　Lǐ Dōngshēng　　　　　shénme　gōngzuò?

⑤ 他 在 一＿＿＿＿＿＿＿＿公司　工作。
　　Tā zài yì　　　　　　　gōngsī gōngzuò.

Choose the right word to fill in the blank (2).

现在	工作	喜欢	每天	哪儿
xiànzài	gōngzuò	xǐhuan	měi tiān	nǎr

① 你 做　什么＿＿＿＿＿＿＿＿?
　　Nǐ　zuò　shénme

② 金　太成 ＿＿＿＿＿＿＿＿下午　来　图书馆。
　　Jīn Tàichéng　　　　　　xiàwǔ lái　túshūguǎn.

③ 玛丽 在＿＿＿＿＿＿＿ 画 画儿?
　　Mǎlì　zài　　　　　　huà huàr?

④ 我　很＿＿＿＿＿＿＿李 老师。
　　Wǒ　hěn　　　　　　Lǐ lǎoshī.

⑤ 经理＿＿＿＿＿＿　不 在 公司。
　　Jīnglǐ　　　　　　bú zài gōngsī.

III. Grammar

Grammar Points

● **Adverbials of time**

Subject + Adverbial of time + Verb (+ Noun)

金　太成　　每天　来　图书馆。
Jīn Tàichéng　měi tiān　lái　túshūguǎn.

她　每天　下午　工作。
Tā　měi tiān　xiàwǔ　gōngzuò.

玛丽　现在　不　工作。
Mǎlì　xiànzài　bù　gōngzuò.

● **Noun/Pronoun+ 的 +Noun**

罗森　的　护照
Luósēn　de　hùzhào

公司　的　职员
gōngsī　de　zhíyuán

我　的　老师
wǒ　de　lǎoshī

● **Adverbials of place**

Subject + Adverbial of place + Verb

他　在一家　公司　工作。
Tā　zài yì jiā　gōngsī　gōngzuò.

我　从　美国　来。
Wǒ　cóng　Měiguó　lái.

● The quantifier　"个，名，家"

Numeral + Quantifier + Noun

一　　个　　中国　人
yí　　ge　　Zhōngguó rén

一　　名　　　大学生
yì　　míng　　dàxuéshēng

一　　家　　公司
yì　　jiā　　gōngsī

1 Put the given word or expression in the right place.

① 金太成　　　A　来 B　公司　C。　　　　（每天 下午）
Jīn Tàichéng　　　lái　gōngsī　　　　měi tiān xiàwǔ

② 他 是 一 家 A　英国　　B　公司　　C　职员。　（的）
Tā shì yì jiā　　Yīngguó　　gōngsī　　zhíyuán　de

③ A　我 爸爸　B　工作　　C。　　　　（在 大学）
　　wǒ bàba　gōngzuò　　　　zài dàxué

④ 山口　和子　A　日本　东京　B　来　C。　（从）
Shānkǒu Hézǐ　　Rìběn Dōngjīng　lái　　cóng

⑤ 张　　圆圆　　　现在　A 是　B 一　C 大学生。
Zhāng Yuányuan　xiànzài　shì　yī　dàxuéshēng.

（名）
míng

2 Complete the following dialogues.

① A: 山口 _____?
　　Shānkǒu

　 B: 她　是　公司　的　　职员。
　　Tā　shì　gōngsī　de　zhíyuán.

② A: 金　太成　　现在_____?
　　Jīn Tàichéng　xiànzài

　 B: 他　现在　在　　中国　　　工作。
　　Tā　xiànzài　zài　Zhōngguó　gōngzuò.

③ A: 王　杨　　在　哪儿　工作?
　　Wáng Yáng　zài　nǎr　gōngzuò?

　 B: _____。

④ A: 这　是　谁　的　护照? / 这是你的护照　吗?
　　Zhè shì shuí de hùzhào? / Zhè shì nǐ de hùzhào ma?

　 B: _____。

⑤ A: 你　每天　下午　来　图书馆　　吗?
　　Nǐ měi tiān xiàwǔ lái túshūguǎn ma?

　 B: _____。

IV. Communication Skills

1 Substitution exercise with the given words.

e.g.　　经理　　　　秘书
　　　　jīnglǐ　　　　mìshū

A:　你 是 <u>经理</u> 吗?
　　Nǐ shì jīnglǐ ma?

B:　不, 我 不 是 经理, 我 是 <u>秘书</u>。
　　Bù, wǒ bú shì jīnglǐ, wǒ shì mìshū.

A:　你 喜欢 这个 工作 吗?
　　Nǐ xǐhuan zhège gōngzuò ma?

B:　对, 我 喜欢 这个 工作。
　　Duì, wǒ xǐhuan zhège gōngzuò.

① 　记者　　　老师
　　jìzhě　　　lǎoshī

A : _____?

B : _____。

A : _____?

B : _____。

② 　职员　　　护士
　　zhíyuán　　hùshi

A : _____?

B：_____。

A：_____？

B：_____。

2 Match the sentences in the two columns to form a conversation.

① 你 喜欢 这个 工作 吗?
Nǐ xǐhuan zhège gōngzuò ma?

A 我 在 一 家
Wǒ zài yì jiā

公司 工作。
gōngsī gōngzuò.

② 她 做 什么 工作?
Tā zuò shénme gōngzuò?

B 不，他 在 大学
Bù, tā zài dàxué

工作。
gōngzuò.

③ 你 在 哪儿 工作?
Nǐ zài nǎr gōngzuò?

C 对，我 妈妈 也
Duì, wǒ māma yě

工作。
gōngzuò.

④ 他 也 在 公司 工作 吗?
Tā yě zài gōngsī gōngzuò ma?

D 她 是 记者。
Tā shì jìzhě.

⑤ 你 妈妈 也 工作 吗?
Nǐ māma yě gōngzuò ma?

E 我 很 喜欢。
Wǒ hěn xǐhuan.

3 Complete the following dialogue.

A： 你＿＿＿＿＿＿＿＿＿＿＿＿＿＿＿＿？
　　 Nǐ

B： 我　在　一　家　美国　　公司　　工作。
　　 Wǒ　zài　yì　jiā　Měiguó　gōngsī　gōngzuò.

A： 你＿＿＿＿＿＿＿＿＿＿＿吗?
　　 Nǐ　　　　　　　　　　　　　ma?

B： 不，我　不　是　经理。
　　 Bù, wǒ　bú　shì　jīnglǐ.

A： 那　你　做＿＿＿＿＿＿＿＿＿＿＿＿？
　　 Nà nǐ zuò

B： 我　　是　经理　的　秘书。
　　 Wǒ　shì　jīnglǐ　de　mìshū.

A： 你　喜欢　你　的　　工作　　吗?
　　 Nǐ　xǐhuan　nǐ　de　gōngzuò　ma?

B： ＿＿＿＿＿＿＿＿＿＿＿＿＿＿＿＿。

V. Chinese Characters

Basic Knowledge

● Basic strokes of Chinese characters (4)

Name of the stroke	Way of writing the stroke	Examples
ㄱ乚 (zhé) Turning stroke	ㄱ (héngzhé) Horizontal turning stroke：Joining the horizontal stroke with the vertical one	日
	乚 (shùzhé) Vertical turning stroke：Joining the vertical stroke with the horizontal one	山

● Basic components of Chinese characters

扌　The radical 扌 (tíshǒu páng)，originally developed from the image of a hand. The original meanings of the characters with 扌 as their radical are generally related to "hand". For example, 护 (hù), 打 (dǎ), 找 (zhǎo).

1 Practise writing the strokes.

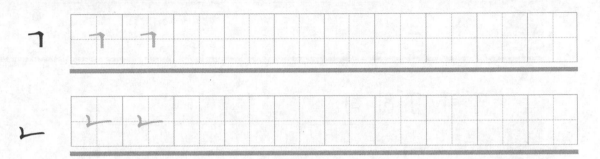

2 Compose the following radicals into characters and form words with them.

① 口　巴　　　（　　　）＿＿＿＿＿＿＿＿＿

　　父　巴　　　（　　　）＿＿＿＿＿＿＿＿＿

② 口　马　　　（　　　）＿＿＿＿＿＿＿＿＿

　　女　马　　　（　　　）＿＿＿＿＿＿＿＿＿

3 Practise writing the characters.

ノ 八 公 公

公 | 公 | 公 | | | | | | | | | | |

フ ㄱ ㄢ 司 司

司 | 司 | 司 | | | | | | | | | | |

一 丁 工

工 | 工 | 工 | | | | | | | | | | |

ノ イ イ 作 作 作 作

作 | 作 | 作 | | | | | | | | | | |

ノ 亡 亡 与 与 每 每 每

每 | 每 | 每 | | | | | | | | | | |

一 二 于 天

天 | 天 | 天 | | | | | | | | | | |

ノ 广 七 午

午 | 午 | 午 | | | | | | | | | | |

一 ナ オ オ 在 在

在 | 在 在

丶 讠 门

门 | 门 门

丿 亻 亻 们 们

们 | 们 们

一 十 士 吉 吉 吉 吉 喜 壴 壴 喜 喜

喜 | 喜 喜

フ ヌ ヌ 欢 欢 欢

欢 | 欢 欢

丶 二 亍 文 文 这 这

这 | 这 这

丿 人 个

个 | 个 个

一 二 千 王 玑 玑 现 现

现 | 现 | 现 | | | | | | | | | | | | |

Unit Five

第五单元

你 今年 多 大
Nǐ jīnnián duō dà

How old are you

Key Points

Subject	Age	
Goals	Learn to ask and tell one's age	
Grammar Points	• The numerals • The special questions with "几" • The noun-predicate sentences • Reduplication of the verb	
Focal Sentences	**Major points in communication**	**Examples**
	Asking and telling a child's age	你今年几岁(了)? ——我四岁(了)。
	Asking and telling an adult's age	你今年多大(了)? ——我 21 岁。
	Asking and telling a senior's age	您今年多大年纪(了)? ——我 65 岁了。
	Making suggestions or enquiring about someone's opinion	你星期六上午来,可以吗?／好吗?
	Identifying someone	您认识这个人吗? 我(不)认识这个人。
Words and Phrases	今年 多大 小朋友 几 岁 猜 对 阿姨 事儿 想 健身 女 星期六 上午 可以 大妈 京剧 声音 真 好听 年纪 外婆 看 赵汉	
Chinese Characters	小 朋 友 今 年 几 岁 猜 对 阿 姨 事 想 健 身 多 女 星 期 六 上 可 以 剧 声 音 真 听 纪 外 婆 看	
Phonetics	Syllable initials: l g x Syllable finals: ang ong iang iong Neutral tone	

Exercises

I . Pronunciation

1 Read the following *Pinyin* aloud and pay attention to their different pronunciations.

bù — pù	bó — pó
duì — tuì	tà — dà
gāo — kāo	guì — kuì
yǒu — yǎo	wài — wàn
pén — péng	gèn — gèng
jīn — jīng	qín — qiú

2 Read the following *Pinyin* aloud and pay attention to their different tones.

qīn	qín	jǐn	jìn
yōu	yóu	yǒu	yòu
jīn	nián	jǐ	suì
měi tiān	hǎotīng	lǎoshī	qǐng wèn

3 Read the following words aloud.

今年	几岁	多大	年纪	朋友	上午	可以
jīnnián	jǐ suì	duō dà	niánjì	péngyou	shàngwǔ	kěyǐ

阿姨	健身	星期	京剧	声音	好听	外婆
āyí	jiànshēn	xīngqī	jīngjù	shēngyīn	hǎotīng	wàipó

Ⅱ.Words and Expressions

1 Pick out the word that does not belong to the group.

① 年纪　　几　　岁　　　　　　　　　　　　（　　　　）
　 niánjì　　jǐ　　suì

② 可以　　今年　　明天　　上午　　　　　　（　　　　）
　 kěyǐ　　jīnnián　míngtiān　shàngwǔ

③ 看　　　事　　　想　　　猜　　　　　　　（　　　　）
　 kàn　　shì　　xiǎng　　cāi

④ 大　　　小　　　几　　　对　　　　　　　（　　　　）
　 dà　　　xiǎo　　jǐ　　　duì

⑤ 大妈　　阿姨　　好听　　外婆　　　　　　（　　　　）
　 dàmā　　āyí　　hǎotīng　wàipó

2 Choose the right word to fill in the blank (1).

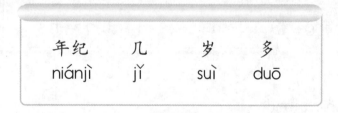

　　年纪　　　　几　　　岁　　　多
　　niánjì　　　jǐ　　　suì　　duō

① 玛丽　今年＿＿＿＿＿＿＿＿＿＿＿大　了?
　 Mǎlì　jīnnián　　　　　　　　　dà　le?

② 山口　　的　　妹妹　　今年＿＿＿＿＿＿＿＿＿岁?
　 Shānkǒu　de　mèimei　jīnnián　　　　　　　suì?

③ 你 外婆 多 大＿＿＿＿＿＿＿＿＿？
Nǐ wàipó duō dà

④ 她 是 护士， 今年 25＿＿＿＿＿＿＿＿＿。
Tā shì hùshi, jīnnián èrshíwǔ

Choose the right word to fill in the blank (2).

好听	真	可以	猜	事儿
hǎotīng	zhēn	kěyǐ	cāi	shìr

① 你＿＿＿＿＿＿＿＿＿她多 大？
Nǐ tā duō dà?

② 你 好! 什么＿＿＿＿＿＿＿＿＿？
Nǐ hǎo! Shénme

③ 赵 老师 的 声音 很＿＿＿＿＿＿＿＿＿。
Zhào lǎoshī de shēngyīn hěn

④ 你们 明天 上午 来 健身，＿＿＿＿＿＿＿＿＿吗？
Nǐmen míngtiān shàngwǔ lái jiànshēn, ma?

⑤ 他 的 年纪＿＿＿＿＿＿＿＿＿大！
Tā de niánjì dà!

Ⅲ. Grammar

Grammar Points

● The numerals 1—10

1	2	3	4	5	6	7	8	9	10
yī	èr	sān	sì	wǔ	liù	qī	bā	jiǔ	shí

21	39	65	83	99
èrshíyī	sānshíjiǔ	liùshíwǔ	bāshísān	jiǔshíjiǔ

● The special questions with "几"

Subject+ Verb + 几 + Classifier + Noun

你 几 岁?
Nǐ jǐ suì?

山口 和子 认识 几 个 中国 朋友?
Shānkǒu Hézǐ rènshi jǐ ge Zhōngguó péngyou?

● The noun-predicate sentences

Subject + Predicate(Noun/Nominal phrase)

我 21 岁。
Wǒ èrshíyī suì.

外婆 今年 83 岁。
Wàipó jīnnián bāshísān suì.

他 法国 人。
Tā Fǎguó rén.

● Reduplication of the verb

Subject + Verb(AA)

我　　看看。
Wǒ　kànkan.

你　　猜猜。
Nǐ　cāicai.

1 Choose the right expression to complete the sentence.

① 小朋友，　　你_____?
　Xiǎopéngyou, nǐ

　A 几岁　　　　　　　B 多　岁
　　jǐ suì　　　　　　　duō suì

② 大妈，　您_____?
　Dàmā, nín

　A 几　年纪　　　　　B 多　大　年纪
　　jǐ niánjì　　　　　　duō dà　niánjì

③ 玛丽，你 认识_____中国　　　学生?
　Mǎlì, nǐ rènshi　　　　　　　Zhōngguó xuésheng?

　A 几　　　　　　　　B 几　个
　　jǐ　　　　　　　　　jǐ　ge

④ 我　猜，你_____。
　Wǒ cāi, nǐ

　A 不　　25　　岁　　B 不　是　25　　岁
　　bú èrshíwǔ suì　　　bú shì èrshíwǔ suì

⑤ 圆圆, 你_____健身 吗?
Yuányuan, nǐ jiànshēn ma?

A 想　　　　　　　　　　B 想想
xiǎng　　　　　　　　　　　xiǎngxiang

2 Complete the following dialogues.

① A:_____?

B: 赵　汉　今年　6　岁。
Zhào Hàn jīnnián liù suì.

② A: _____?

B: 我　猜　他　30　岁。
Wǒ cāi tā sānshí suì.

③ A: _____?

B: 我　爸爸　今年　60　岁。
Wǒ bàba jīnnián liùshí suì.

④ A: 你　明天　上午　来, 可以　吗?
Nǐ míngtiān shàngwǔ lái, kěyǐ ma?

B: _____。

⑤ A: (Pointing a photo) 你　认识　这个　人　吗?
Nǐ rènshi zhège rén ma?

B: _____。(Verb AA)

IV. Communication Skills

1 Look at the pictures and complete the dialogues with the given words.

①

A: _____? （几）

B: _____。

②

25岁

A: _____? （多大）

B: _____。

③

A: _____? （多大）

B: _____。

④

A: _____? （认识）

B: _____。

⑤

A: _____? （看看）

B: _____。

2 Complete the following dialogues.

① A: 你 好， 你 想＿＿＿＿＿＿＿＿？
　　Nǐ hǎo, nǐ xiǎng

B: 我 想 健身。
　Wǒ xiǎng jiànshēn.

A: 你＿＿＿＿＿＿＿？
　Nǐ

B: 我 今年 21 岁。
　Wǒ jīnnián èrshíyī suì.

A: 你 星期六 上午 来，＿＿＿＿＿＿吗？
　Nǐ xīngqīliù shàngwǔ lái, 　　　　　ma?

B: 可以。
　Kěyǐ.

② A: 大妈， 您 好。您＿＿＿＿＿＿＿＿？
　　Dàmā, nín hǎo. Nín

B: 我 今年 83 岁。
　Wǒ jīnnián bāshísān suì.

A: 请 问，（Pointing the photo）你＿＿＿＿这个 人 吗?
　Qǐng wèn, 　　　　　nǐ 　　　　zhège rén ma?

B: 我＿＿＿＿＿＿，不 认识。 她 是……
　Wǒ 　　　　　bú rènshi. Tā shì……

A: 我 妈妈 的 妈妈。
　Wǒ māma de māma.

B: 哦， 是 你＿＿＿＿＿＿啊。
　Ò, shì nǐ 　　　　　a.

V. Chinese Characters

Basic Knowledge

● Basic order of the strokes of Chinese characters (1).

Basic order of strokes	Example and way of writing the stroke
First the horizontal one then the vertical one	十： 一 十
From top to bottom	三： 一 二 三
First left-falling then right-falling	人： 丿 人
First the left one then the right one	儿： 丿 儿

● Basic components of Chinese characters

心　It appears at the bottom of the characters with a top-bottom structure, generally known as 心字底 (xīn zì dǐ) (the radical 心 used at the bottom of a character). It is originally developed from the image of a heart. The original meanings of the characters with 心 as their radical are generally related to thoughts and feelings. For example, 想 (xiǎng), 您 (nín), 意 (yì), 思 (sī).

丝　　It appears on the left side of the characters with a left-right structure, generally known as 绞丝旁 (the radical 丝 jiǎosī páng). For example, 给 (gěi), 绍 (shào), 练 (liàn), 经 (jīng), 纪 (jì), 线 (xiàn), 结 (jié).

1 Compose the following radicals into characters and form words with them.

① 相　　心　　（　　　　）＿＿＿＿＿＿＿＿＿

你　　心　　（　　　　）＿＿＿＿＿＿＿＿＿

② 丝　　合　　（　　　　）＿＿＿＿＿＿＿＿＿

丝　　召　　（　　　　）＿＿＿＿＿＿＿＿＿

丝　　己　　（　　　　）＿＿＿＿＿＿＿＿＿

2 Practise writing the characters.

丿 小 小

小	小	小						

丿 几 月 月 朋 朋 朋 朋

朋	朋	朋						

一 ナ 方 友

| 友 | 友 | 友 | | | | | | | | | | | |

ノ 人 仐 今

| 今 | 今 | 今 | | | | | | | | | | | |

ノ ノ ヒ 乍 午 年

| 年 | 年 | 年 | | | | | | | | | | | |

ノ 几

| 几 | 几 | 几 | | | | | | | | | | | |

丨 屵 屵 屵 岁 岁

| 岁 | 岁 | 岁 | | | | | | | | | | | |

ノ 亻 亻 白 自 身 身

| 身 | 身 | 身 | | | | | | | | | | | |

丶 讠 讠 讠 讠 讠 讠 讠 谢 谢

| 谢 | 谢 | 谢 | | | | | | | | | | | |

㇉ ㇇ ㇇ ㇇ 多 多

多	多	多												

丨 上 上

上	上	上												

一 丆 丆 口 可

可	可	可												

丶 丷 以 以

以	以	以												

丨 冂 口 口 吖 听 听

听	听	听												

一 二 三 手 看 看 看 看 看

看	看	看												

Unit Six

第六单元

她 的 男朋友 很 帅
Tā de nánpéngyou hěn shuài

Her boyfriend is very handsome

Key Points

Subject	One's figure and features
Goals	Learn to tell in simple terms about one's height, weight and general appearance
Grammar Points	● The alternative questions ● Questions with "多+Adjective" ● The positive-negative questions ● Sentences with an adjectival predicate; adverbs of degree

Focal Sentences	Major points in communication	Examples
	Talking about someone's appearance	他帅不帅？ 他很帅。
	Talking about someone's height and weight	她1米65。 我体重54公斤。
	Asking someone's wishes：想+ Verb phrase +吗？	你想找这样的男朋友吗？

Words and Phrases	男朋友 帅 怎么样 不错 外国人 大学 学习 男 个子 高 米 左右 找 这样 小姐 累 明天 休息 要 太 胖 体重 公斤 还可以 那 漂亮 外公 汉语
Chinese Characters	怎 样 错 习 汉 语 男 子 米 左 右 帅 找 样 男 姐 累 明 天 休 息 要 太 胖 体 重 公 斤 还 那 时 漂 亮
Phonetics	Syllable initials: j　q Syllable finals: ü　er　in　ing Retroflextion

Exercises

Ⅰ. Pronunciation

1 Read the following *Pinyin* aloud and pay attention to their different pronunciations.

jiào — qiào		jiāng — qiāng	
zuǒ — zǒu		xiān — xiāng	
nián — lián		liáng — niáng	
bān — bāng		zěn — zēng	
yān — yāng		yāo — yōu	
fān — fēn		dāng — dēng	

2 Read the following *Pinyin* aloud and pay attention to their different tones.

kē	xué	zuǒ	yòu
bāng	máng	qǐng	jià
zhēn	lái	xiǎng	duì
bù tīng	bù lái	bù zǒu	bú kàn

3 Read the following words aloud.

怎么样	不错	外国	大学	学习	汉语	还是	那时
zěnmeyàng	búcuò	wàiguó	dàxué	xuéxí	Hànyǔ	háishi	nàshí

个子	左右	这样	明天	休息	体重	公斤	漂亮
gèzi	zuǒyòu	zhèyàng	míngtiān	xiūxi	tǐzhòng	gōngjīn	piàoliang

Ⅱ.Words and Expressions

1 Pick out the word that does not belong to the group.

① 高　　帅　　胖　　找　　　　（　　　）
　　gāo　shuài　pàng　zhǎo

② 外公　　外婆　　这样　　小姐　　　（　　　）
　　wàigōng　wàipó　zhèyàng　xiǎojie

③ 不错　　个子　　外国　　体重　　　（　　　）
　　búcuò　gèzi　wàiguó　tǐzhòng

④ 明天　　左右　　现在　　怎么样　　（　　　）
　　míngtiān　zuǒyòu　xiànzài　zěnmeyàng

⑤ 学习　　找　　漂亮　　休息　　　（　　　）
　　xuéxí　zhǎo　piàoliang　xiūxi

2 Choose the right word to fill in the blank (1).

米	漂亮	公斤	累	帅
mǐ	piàoliang	gōngjīn	lèi	shuài

① 张　　圆圆　　的　　教练　　很＿＿＿＿＿＿＿＿。
　　Zhāng Yuányuan　de　jiàoliàn　hěn

② 他　　体重　　80＿＿＿＿＿＿＿＿。
　　Tā　tǐzhòng　bāshí

③ 她　的　外婆　那时　很＿＿＿＿＿＿＿＿＿＿。
　Tā　de　wàipó　nàshí　hěn

④ 我　很＿＿＿＿＿＿＿＿＿，　我　想　休息。
　Wǒ　hěn　　　　　　　　　wǒ　xiǎng　xiūxi.

⑤ 我　个子　不　高，　1＿＿＿＿＿＿＿＿＿70。
　Wǒ　gèzi　bù　gāo, yì　　　　　　　qī líng.

Choose the right word to fill in the blank (2).

左右	怎么样	这样	休息	还是
zuǒyòu	zěnmeyàng	zhèyàng	xiūxi	háishi

① 你　的　汉语　老师＿＿＿＿＿＿＿＿？
　Nǐ　de　Hànyǔ　lǎoshī

② 他　1　米　75　＿＿＿＿＿＿＿＿。
　Tā　yì　mǐ　qī wǔ

③ 我　不　想　要＿＿＿＿＿＿＿的　男朋友。
　Wǒ　bù　xiǎng　yào　　　　　　de　nánpéngyou.

④ 你　是　美国　人＿＿＿＿＿＿＿英国　人?
　Nǐ　shì　Měiguó rén　　　　　　Yīngguó　rén?

⑤ 我　太　累了，明天　想＿＿＿＿＿＿＿。
　Wǒ　tài　lèi le, míngtiān　xiǎng

Ⅲ. Grammar

Grammar Points

● **The alternative questions**

Subject（+是）+ Phrase + 还 + Phrase

星期六　　　　你　休息　还是　学习？
Xīngqīliù　　　nǐ　xiūxi　háishi　xuéxí?

玛丽　是　美国　人　还是　英国　人？
Mǎlì　shì　Měiguó　rén　háishi　Yīngguó　rén?

● **Questions with the "多+Adjective" construction**

Subject + 多 + Adjective

他　多　高？
Tā　duō　gāo?

● **The positive-negative questions**

Subject + Adjective/Verb + 不 + Adjective/Verb

他　高　不　高？
Tā　gāo　bu　gāo?

你　去　不　去？
Nǐ　qù　bu　qù?

● The adjectival-predicate sentences and the adverbs of degree

Subject　+　Adverb +　Adjective

我　　的 老师　　很　　好。
Wǒ　de　lǎoshī　hěn　hǎo.

他　　很　　胖。
Tā　hěn　pàng.

Subject　+　　Adverb +　Adjective　+　了

她　　太　　漂亮　　　　了！
Tā　tài　piàoliang　le!

你　的　教练　　真　　帅！
Nǐ　de　jiàoliàn　zhēn　shuài!

1　Transform the following sentences into their interrogative form (1).

e.g. 我　去　　图书馆。
　　　Wǒ　qù　túshūguǎn.

　　　→你　去 不 去　　图书馆?
　　　　Nǐ　qù bu qù　túshūguǎn?

① 他 的　女朋友　　很　　漂亮。
　 Tā de nǚpéngyou hěn piàoliang.

　 →_____?

② 她 很　高兴。
　 Tā hěn gāoxìng.

　 →_____?

③ 我　很　累。
Wǒ　hěn　lèi.

→_____?

④ 他　明天　休息。
Tā　míngtiān　xiūxi.

→_____?

⑤ 我　看　京剧。
Wǒ　kàn　jīngjù.

→_____?

Transform the following sentences into their interrogative form (2).

e.g.　玛丽　是　英国　人。
　　　Mǎlì　shì　Yīngguó rén.

→玛丽　是　美国　人　还是　英国　人?　（美国人 Měiguó rén）
　Mǎlì　shì　Měiguó rén háishi　Yīngguó rén?

① 我的　教练　是　男的。
Wǒ de　jiàoliàn　shì　nán de.

→_____?　（女的 nǚ de）

② 明天　我　休息。
Míngtiān　wǒ　xiūxi.

→_____?　（学习 xuéxí）

③ 金　太成　是　经理。
Jīn　Tàichéng　shì　jīnglǐ.

→ _____? （职员 zhíyuán）

④ 我　　喜欢　　北京。
Wǒ　xǐhuan　Běijīng.

→ _____? （上海 Shànghǎi）

⑤ 我　　星期六　　上午　　来。
Wǒ　xīngqīliù　shàngwǔ　lái.

→ _____?（星期六下午 xīngqīliù xiàwǔ）

2 Complete the following dialogues with the given words or expressions.

① A: _____? （多 duō）

B: 他　1 米　73。
Tā　yì mǐ　qī sān.

② A: _____? （多 duō）

B: 我　　56　　公斤。
Wǒ　wǔshíliù　gōngjīn.

③ A: 张　　圆圆　　漂亮　　不　　漂亮?
Zhāng Yuányuan　piàoliang　bu　piàoliang?

B: _____。（很 hěn）

④ A: 你　的　教练　　怎么样?
Nǐ　de　jiàoliàn　zěnmeyàng?

B: _____! （太……了 tài ……le）

⑤ A: 他　体重　　85　　公斤。
Tā tǐzhòng　bāshíwǔ　gōngjīn.

B: _____! （真 zhēn）

IV. Communication Skills

1 Mark the pictures with the number of the corresponding descriptions.

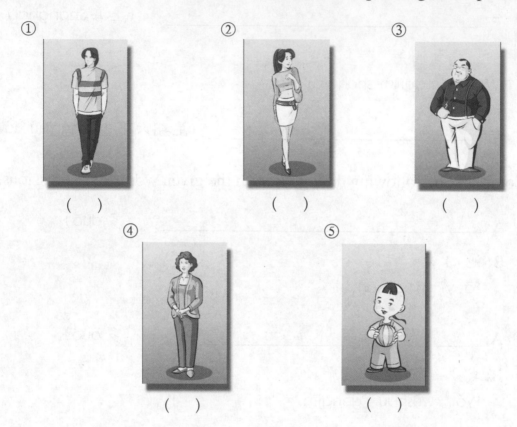

① ( ) ② ( ) ③ ( )

④ ( ) ⑤ ( )

A 他 个子 不 高， 体重 75 公斤， 很 胖。
  Tā gèzi bù gāo, tǐzhòng qīshíwǔ gōngjīn, hěn pàng.

B 她 身高 1米65， 体重 45 公斤， 很
  Tā shēngāo yì mǐ liù wǔ, tǐzhòng sìshíwǔ gōngjīn, hěn

  漂亮。
  piàoliang.

C 他 今年 6岁， 身高 1米2， 体重 20
  Tā jīnnián liù suì, shēngāo yì mǐ èr, tǐzhòng èrshí

  公斤 左右。
  gōngjīn zuǒyòu.

D 他　个子　很　高，　1　米　78　左右，很　帅。
Tā　gèzi　hěn gāo,　yì　mǐ　qī bā　zuǒyòu, hěn　shuài.

E 她　今年　65　岁，体重　60　公斤，　不　太　胖。
Tā　jīnnián liùshíwǔ　suì,　tǐzhòng　liùshí　gōngjīn,　bú　tài　pàng.

2 Complete the following dialogues according to the given information in the boxes.

姓名：张圆圆
职业：大学生
年龄：21岁
身高：1.65米
体重：45公斤
健身时间：星期六下午

① A: 你_____不_____？
　　 Nǐ　　　　 bù

B: 我　是　　大学生。
　 Wǒ　shì　dàxuéshēng.

A: _____?

B: 我　1　米　　65。
　 Wǒ　yì　mǐ　liù wǔ.

A: _____?

B: 我　体重　45　　公斤。
　 Wǒ　tǐzhòng　sìshíwǔ　gōngjīn.

A: 你_____还是_____?
　　 Nǐ　　　　　　 háishi

B: 我　星期六　下午　来。
　 Wǒ　xīngqīliù　xiàwǔ　lái.

姓名：刘小飞
职业：大学教师
年龄：28岁
身高：1.78米
体重：70公斤
健身时间：星期六上午

② A: 他 是 不 是 学生？
　　Tā shì bu shì xuésheng?

B: ＿＿＿＿＿＿＿＿＿＿。

A: 他＿＿＿＿＿＿不＿＿＿＿＿＿？
　　Tā　　　　　bù

B: 他 真 帅！
　　Tā zhēn shuài!

A: ＿＿＿＿＿＿＿＿＿＿＿＿＿＿？

B: 他 今年 28 岁。
　　Tā　jīnnián èrshíbā suì.

A: 你＿＿＿＿＿＿＿＿吗？
　　Nǐ　　　　　　　ma?

B: 当然 想。
　　Dāngrán xiǎng.

V. Chinese Characters

Basic Knowledge

● Basic order of strokes of Chinese characters (2).

Basic order of strokes	Example and way of writing the stroke
First the middle then the left and the right	小：丿 小 小
First the external then the internal	同：冂 冂 同
First the inside strokes then the horizontal one to seal it	国：冂 国 国

● Basic components of Chinese characters

氵 The radical 氵(sān diǎn shuǐ páng). The original meanings of the characters with 氵 as their radical are generally related to "water". For example, 汉 (hàn), 没 (mò), 漂 (piāo), 江 (jiāng), 河 (hé), 海 (hǎi), 洋 (yáng).

木 The radical 木 (mù zì páng) is originally developed from the image of a tree. The original meanings of the characters with 木 as their radical are generally related to "tree". For example, 林 (lín), 样 (yàng), 树 (shù).

1 Compose the following radicals into characters and form words with them.

① 氵　　殳　　（　　）　_____

　　氵　　又　　（　　）　_____

　　氵　　票　　（　　）　_____

② 亻　　木　　（　　）　_____

　　木　　羊　　（　　）　_____

③ 相　　心　　（　　）　_____

　　你　　心　　（　　）　_____

　　乍　　心　　（　　）　_____

　　自　　心　　（　　）　_____

2 Practise writing the characters.

丿 亻 仁 午 午 乍 怎 怎 怎

| 怎 | 怎 | 怎 | | | | | | | | | | | | |

一 十 十 木 术 术 栏 栏 栏 样

| 样 | 样 | 样 | | | | | | | | | | | | |

フ ヲ 习

| 习 | 习 | 习 | | | | | | | | | | | | |

丶 冫 氵 汈 汉

| 汉 | 汉 | 汉 | | | | | | | | | | | | |

丶 讠 讠 讠 语 语 语 语

| 语 | 语 | 语 | | | | | | | | | | | | |

丨 冂 日 田 田 罗 男

| 男 | 男 | 男 | | | | | | | | | | | | |

一 丁 疒 不 还 还 还

| 还 | 还 | 还 | | | | | | | | | | | |

フ 了 子

| 子 | 子 | 子 | | | | | | | | | | | |

丶 丷 丷 半 米 米

| 米 | 米 | 米 | | | | | | | | | | | |

一 ナ 广 左 左

| 左 | 左 | 左 | | | | | | | | | | | |

一 ナ 才 右 右

| 右 | 右 | 右 | | | | | | | | | | | |

く 女 女 如 如 如 姐 姐

| 姐 | 姐 | 姐 | | | | | | | | | | | |

丨 冂 冃 日 町 明 明 明

| 明 | 明 | 明 | | | | | | | | | | | |

ノイイ什休休

| 休 | 休 | 休 | | | | | | | | | | |

ノイヤ白白自息息息

| 息 | 息 | 息 | | | | | | | | | | |

一一一一而西要要

| 要 | 要 | 要 | | | | | | | | | | |

一ナ大太

| 太 | 太 | 太 | | | | | | | | | | |

ノイイ什休休体

| 体 | 体 | 体 | | | | | | | | | | |

１ 冂 日 日 旷 时 时

| 时 | 时 | 时 | | | | | | | | | | |

Unit Seven

第七单元

我 住 在 阳光 小区
Wǒ zhù zài Yángguāng Xiǎoqū

I live in Yangguang Residential District

Key Points

Subject	Addresses
Goals	Learn to tell one's location and address
Grammar Points	• The expression of ordinal numbers • The expression of direction or locality • The "A＋离＋B＋远／近" structure

Focal Sentences	Major points in communication	Examples
	Asking or telling someone's address	你住在哪儿？ ——我住在阳光小区24号楼17层1708号。
	Asking or telling a distance	第二医院离这儿远不远？ ——不太远。
	Responding to thanks	别客气。
	Bidding goodbye	一会儿见。 明天见。

Words and Phrases	住 我们 学校 有 健美操 比赛 参加 当 去 宿舍 号 楼 房间 电话 见 喂 家 里 今天 晚上 宴会 饭店 小区 接 层 前边 等 一会儿 第二 医院 路 离 这儿 远 知道 东边 别客气（别、客气） 长安饭店 阳光小区 第二医院 东城路

Chinese Characters	校 有 美 操 比 赛 参 加 当 去 住 宿 舍 号 楼 房 间 电 话 见 喂 里 晚 宴 会 饭 店 区 接 层 前 边 等 医 院 路 离 远 知 道 东 别 客 气

Phonetics	Syllable initials：s k Syllable finals：ou ia iou eng Combination of tones

Exercises

Ⅰ. Pronunciation

1 Read the following *Pinyin* aloud and pay attention to their different pronunciations.

zǐ —— cǐ		zuò —— cuò	
jiǎo —— qiǎo		jiàn —— qiàn	
zuì —— cuì		jǐ —— qǐ	
wǔ —— yǔ		wàn —— wàng	
yè —— yuè		dàn —— duàn	
wēi —— wēn		fēi —— fēn	

2 Read the following *Pinyin* aloud and pay attention to their different tones.

wān	wán	wǎn	wàn
yuē	wéi	yǔ	wèn
ān	quán	bǐ	sài
fēi	cháng	kě	ài

3 Read the following words aloud.

我们	学校	宿舍	房间	电话	知道	前边
wǒmen	xuéxiào	sùshè	fángjiān	diànhuà	zhīdao	qiánbian

晚上	饭店	医院	宴会	健美操	比赛	客气
wǎnshang	fàndiàn	yīyuàn	yànhuì	jiànměicāo	bǐsài	kèqi

Ⅱ.Words and Expressions

1 Pick out the word that does not belong to the group.

① 知道　　参加　　饭店　　喜欢　　　　　（　　　）
　 zhīdao　cānjiā　fàndiàn　xǐhuan

② 当　　　号　　　去　　　住　　　　　　　（　　　）
　 dāng　　hào　　qù　　　zhù

③ 离　　　有　　　从　　　在　　　　　　　（　　　）
　 lí　　　yǒu　　cóng　　zài

④ 住　　　楼　　　层　　　号　　　　　　　（　　　）
　 zhù　　lóu　　céng　　hào

⑤ 别客气　　没关系　　对不起　　一会儿　　（　　　）
　 bié kèqi　méi guānxi　duìbuqǐ　yíhuìr

2 Choose the right word to fill in the blank (1).

住　　　当　　　接　　　参加　　　有
zhù　　dāng　　jiē　　cānjiā　　yǒu

① 菲雅　喜欢_____记者。
　 Fēiyǎ　xǐhuan　　　　　　　　　　jìzhě.

② 你_____健美操　比赛　吗?
　 Nǐ　　　　　　　　jiànměicāo　bǐsài　ma?

③ 星期六　　晚上　　我　去＿＿＿＿＿＿＿＿你。
　　Xīngqīliù　wǎnshang　wǒ qù　　　　　　　　　nǐ.

④ 我＿＿＿＿＿＿＿＿在　　学生　　宿舍。
　　Wǒ　　　　　　　zài　xuésheng　sùshè.

⑤ 明天　　　我们　　学校＿＿＿＿＿＿＿健美操　　比赛。
　　Míngtiān　wǒmen　xuéxiào　　　　　　jiànměicāo　bǐsài.

Choose the right word to fill in the blank (2).

离	里	饭店	前边	晚上
lí	lǐ	fàndiàn	qiánbian	wǎnshang

① 长安　＿＿＿＿＿＿＿＿在　东城　路，很　近。
　　Cháng'ān　　　　　　zài Dōngchéng Lù, hěn jìn.

② 我　在　家＿＿＿＿＿＿＿。你来接我吧。
　　Wǒ zài jiā　　　　　　Nǐ lái jiē wǒ ba.

③ 王　杨　家＿＿＿＿＿＿＿公司　很　远。
　　Wáng Yáng jiā　　　　　gōngsī hěn yuǎn.

④ 2 号　楼　在 3 号　楼＿＿＿＿＿＿＿。
　　Èr hào lóu zài sān hào lóu

⑤ 今天＿＿＿＿＿＿＿我去　健身。
　　Jīntiān　　　　　wǒ qù jiànshēn.

Ⅲ. Grammar

Grammar Points

● The expression of ordinal numbers.

她	住	在	12	号	楼	15	层	1506
Tā	zhù	zài	shí'èr	hào	lóu	shíwǔ	céng	yāo wǔ líng liù

号　房间。
hào fángjiān.

第二　医院　很　远。
Dì-èr Yīyuàn hěn yuǎn.

● The expression of direction or locality

Subject + 在 + direction/locality

我们	学校	在	长安	饭店	东边。
Wǒmen	xuéxiào	zài	Cháng'ān	Fàndiàn	dōngbian.

菲雅　在　玛丽　前边。
Fēiyǎ zài Mǎlì qiánbian.

● The "A + 离 + B + 远／近" structure

Subject　+ 离 + Object + 远／近

你	家	离	公司	远	吗?
Nǐ	jiā	lí	gōngsī	yuǎn	ma?

阳光	小区	离	这儿	不	远。
Yángguāng	Xiǎoqū	lí	zhèr	bù	yuǎn.

1 Put the given word in the right place.

① 他 住 在 8 A 楼 9 B 903 　C 房间。　　（层）
　 Tā zhù zài bā lóu jiǔ jiǔ líng sān fángjiān.　　céng

② 他 爸爸 　A 　现在 住 在 B 二 C 医院。　　（第）
　 Tā bàba 　　xiànzài zhù zài 　　èr 　Yīyuàn.　　dì

③ 请 问, 　A 长安 　饭店 B 这儿 C 远 吗?
　 Qǐng wèn, 　　Cháng'ān Fàndiàn 　zhèr 　yuǎn ma?
　　　　　　　　　　　　　　　　　　　　　　　　　（离）
　　　　　　　　　　　　　　　　　　　　　　　　　lí

④ 我们 　A 公司 在 　B 阳光 　小区 C。　　（东边）
　 Wǒmen 　gōngsī zài 　　Yángguāng Xiǎoqū 　　dōngbian

⑤ 张 　圆圆 　A 　现在 在 B 宿舍 C。　　（里）
　 Zhāng Yuányuan 　　xiànzài zài 　sùshè 　　lǐ

2 Fill in each blank with the proper preposition.

在	离	从
zài	lí	cóng

① 我 爸爸＿＿＿＿一家 公司 工作。
　 Wǒ bàba 　　　yì jiā gōngsī gōngzuò.

② 学校 ＿＿＿＿ 我们 小区 不 远。
　 Xuéxiào 　　wǒmen xiǎoqū bù yuǎn.

③ 山口　和子 _____ 日本　东京　来。
Shānkǒu Hézǐ　　　Rìběn　Dōngjīng　lái.

④ 图书馆 _____ 2 号　楼 的　东边。
Túshūguǎn　　　èr hào lóu de dōngbian.

⑤ 我 _____ 宿舍楼　前边　等　你。
Wǒ　　　　sùshèlóu qiánbian děng nǐ.

IV. Communication Skills

1　Complete the following dialogues according to the pictures.

① A: 圆圆，_____?
Yuányuan,

B: 我　住 在_____。
Wǒ zhù zài

A: 现在　我　去　找　你。
Xiànzài wǒ qù zhǎo nǐ.

B: 我　在　宿舍　等　你。
Wǒ zài sùshè děng nǐ.

A: 好，_____。
Hǎo,

B: _____。

② A: 请问, _____?
Qǐng wèn,

   B: 在_____。
Zài

   A: 离_____?
Lí

   B: 不_____。
Bù

   A: 谢谢 你!
Xièxie nǐ!

   B: _____。

2 Substitute the underlined parts according to your real situation.

   A: 你 住 在 哪儿?
   Nǐ zhù zài nǎr?

   B: 我 住 在 阳光 小区。
   Wǒ zhù zài Yángguāng Xiǎoqū.

   A: 你们 学校／公司 在 哪儿?
   Nǐmen xuéxiào/gōngsī zài nǎr?

   B: 在 东城 路。
   Zài Dōngchéng Lù.

   A: 你 家 离 学校／公司 远 吗?
   Nǐ jiā lí xuéxiào/gōngsī yuǎn ma?

   B: 不 太 远。
   Bú tài yuǎn.

Ⅴ. Chinese Characters

Basic Knowledge

● The number of strokes of Chinese characters

The number of strokes of each Chinese character is fixed, which has the function of distinguishing the shape of a character. If you write more or less strokes, you may have the character wrongly written. For example,

人 (2 strokes) —— 大 (3 strokes)

大 (3 strokes) —— 太 (4 strokes)

大 (3 strokes) —— 夫 (4 strokes)

口 (3 strokes) —— 中 (4 strokes)

王 (4 strokes) —— 玉 (5 strokes)

● Basic components of Chinese characters

宀 The radical 宀 (bǎo gài tóu) used at the top of a character, originally developed from the image of a house. It appears on the top of characters with a top-bottom structure. The original meanings of the characters with 宀 as their radical are generally related to "house". For example, 家 (jiā), 宿 (sù), 客 (kè), 宴 (yàn), 室 (shì).

辶 The radical 辶 (zǒu zhī páng). The original meanings of the characters with 辶 as their radical are generally related to "walking". For example，边 (biān), 还 (hái), 远 (yuǎn), 近 (jìn), 道 (dào), 遍 (biàn), 过 (guò), 进 (jìn), 送 (sòng).

1 Figure out the number of strokes of the characters in each group.

人 (_____strokes)   大 (_____strokes)

大 (_____strokes)   太 (_____strokes)

大 (_____strokes)   儿 (_____strokes)

天 (_____strokes)   几 (_____strokes)

工 (_____strokes)

士 (_____strokes)

2 Compose the following radicals into characters and form words with them.

① 宀   豕   (   )_____

宀   各   (   )_____

宀   亻   百   (   )_____

② 辶   力   (   )_____

辶   不   (   )_____

辶   元   (   )_____

辶   首   (   )_____

辶   扁   (   )_____

3 Practise writing the characters.

一 ナ 才 冇 冇 有

有	有	有												

一 Ł Ł 比

比	比	比												

一 十 土 去 去

去	去	去												

ノ 亻 亻 亻 伫 住 住

住	住	住												

丨 口 口 号 号

号	号	号												

丶 亠 亠 户 户 序 房 房

房	房	房												

` 丨门 门 问 问 问

间 | 间 | 间 |

` 丨门门 门 问 问 问

丨 冂 冃 日 电

电 | 电 | 电 |

` 讠 讠 讠 话 话 话 话

话 | 话 | 话 |

丨 冂 贝 见

见 | 见 | 见 |

丨 冂 冃 日 旦 甲 里

里 | 里 | 里 |

丿 人 公 会 会 会

会 | 会 | 会 |

丿 饣 饣 饣 饣 饭 饭

饭 | 饭 | 饭 |

丶 亠 广 广 庁 庄 店 店

| 店 | 店 | 店 | | | | | | | | | | | |

フ 力 力 边 边

| 边 | 边 | 边 | | | | | | | | | | | |

一 丆 丆 三 至 医 医

| 医 | 医 | 医 | | | | | | | | | | | |

´ 阝 阝 阝 阝 阡 阡 陀 院

| 院 | 院 | 院 | | | | | | | | | | | |

丨 口 口 口 尸 尸 足 足 趵 政 政 路 路

| 路 | 路 | 路 | | | | | | | | | | | |

一 二 亍 元 元 远 远

| 远 | 远 | 远 | | | | | | | | | | | |

丿 仁 仁 午 矢 知 知 知

| 知 | 知 | 知 | | | | | | | | | | | |

`、 丶 丷 丷 广 芦 芦 首 首 首 道 道`

道	道	道											

`一 七 듁 东 东`

东	东	东											

`丶 冂 口 号 另 别 别`

别	别	别											

`丶 丷 宀 宀 岁 安 安 客 客`

客	客	客											

`丿 丿 乞 气`

气	气	气											

Unit Eight

第八单元

我 喜欢 大 家庭
Wǒ xǐhuan dà jiātíng

I like an extended family

Key Points

Subject	Family
Goals	Learn to ask/tell briefly about family members
Grammar Points	• The "有" sentences indicating possession • The sentence tag "了" • The expression of "only": 只有 • The construction "和……一起／一个人" as an adverbial

Focal Sentences	Major points in communication	Examples
	Asking or telling about family members	你家(有)几口人? ——我家(有)四口人。
	Telling someone's wishes	我爸爸希望我去银行工作。
	Telling about one's feeling of something	这个小区真漂亮。 真是个大家庭。

Words and Phrases	家庭 家 口 四 妹妹 和 律师 忙 非常 常常 希望 银行 可是 大夫 兄弟姐妹 (兄弟、姐妹) 只 孩子 呢 姐姐 双胞胎 前面 送 父母 一起 家人 都 爷爷 奶奶 哥哥 嫂子 他们 一共 家庭
Chinese Characters	口 四 妹 和 律 忙 常 希 望 银 行 大 夫 兄 弟 只 孩 呢 双 胞 胎 面 送 父 母 起 都 爷 奶 哥 嫂 共 庭
Phonetics	Syllable initials: z c Syllable finals: iao ian ua uai Combination of tones

Exercises

I . Pronunciation

1 Read the following *Pinyin* aloud and pay attention to their different pronunciations.

zài	—	cài		zuì	—	cuì	
zhè	—	chè		zhōng	—	chōng	
zāi	—	zhāi		zhǎo	—	zǎo	
cā	—	chā		cháng	—	cáng	
wāng	—	wēng		huáng	—	hóng	
zhuān	—	zhuāng		wèn	—	wèng	

2 Read the following *Pinyin* aloud and pay attention to their different tones.

zhī	zhí	zhǐ	zhì
wāng	wáng	wǎng	wàng
dōng	yáng	zhǎo	gòng
fā	huáng	chǎo	cài

3 Read the following words aloud.

父母	哥哥	嫂子	兄弟	姐姐	妹妹
fùmǔ	gēge	sǎozi	xiōngdì	jiějie	mèimei

家庭	孩子	一共	还有	一起	前面
jiātíng	háizi	yígòng	háiyǒu	yìqǐ	qiánmian

II. Words and Expressions

1 Pick out the word that does not belong to the group.

① 姐姐　　妹妹　　哥哥　　姐妹　　　　（　　）
　jiějie　mèimei　gēge　jiěmèi

② 还有　　一共　　一起　　常常　　　　（　　）
　háiyǒu　yígòng　yìqǐ　chángcháng

③ 家庭　　家人　　家　　　和　　　　　（　　）
　jiātíng　jiārén　jiā　　hé

④ 送　　　想　　　忙　　　希望　　　　（　　）
　sòng　xiǎng　máng　xīwàng

⑤ 律师　　银行　　大夫　　职员　　　　（　　）
　lùshī　yínháng　dàifu　zhíyuán

2 Choose the right word to fill in the blank.

金　太成　是　韩国　学生。　他_①_有　爷爷、奶奶、
Jīn Tàichéng shì Hánguó xuésheng.　Tā　yǒu　yéye、nǎinai、

爸爸、妈妈、哥哥、嫂子、_②_哥哥　嫂子　的　孩子，_③_ 10_④_
bàba、māma、gēge、sǎozi、　　gēge sǎozi de háizi,　　　shí

人。他们　都　住　在_⑤_，真　是　个　大_⑥_。
rén. Tāmen dōu zhù zài　　zhēn shì ge dà

现在　金　太成　在　北京　学习，他　很_⑦_家。
Xiànzài Jīn Tàichéng zài Běijīng xuéxí, tā hěn　jiā.

① A 家　　　B 家人　　　C 家庭
　　jiā　　　　 jiārén　　　　jiātíng

② A 有　　　B 还有　　　C 还是
　　yǒu　　　　hái yǒu　　　háishi

③ A 都　　　B 一共　　　C 一起
　　dōu　　　　yígòng　　　 yìqǐ

④ A 名　　　B 口　　　　C 家
　　míng　　　 kǒu　　　　　jiā

⑤ A 都　　　B 一共　　　C 一起
　　dōu　　　　yígòng　　　 yìqǐ

⑥ A 家　　　B 家人　　　C 家庭
　　jiā　　　　 jiārén　　　　jiātíng

⑦ A 想　　　B 要　　　　C 希望
　　xiǎng　　　yào　　　　　xīwàng

3 Choose the right word to fill in the blank.

只　　忙　　和　　送　　都
zhǐ　 máng　 hé　 sòng　 dōu

① 他 不 是 经理, 可是 他 每天　都　很＿＿＿＿＿＿＿＿＿。
　Tā bú shì jīnglǐ, kěshì tā měi tiān　dōu hěn

② 你 住 在 哪儿? 我＿＿＿＿＿＿＿＿你 好 吗?
　Nǐ zhù zài nǎr? Wǒ　　　　　　　　 nǐ hǎo ma?

③ 张 芳芳 ＿＿＿＿＿＿＿ 张 圆圆 是 双胞胎。
Zhāng Fāngfāng　　　　　　　 Zhāng Yuányuan shì shuāngbāotāi.

④ 我　　没有　　兄弟 姐妹。　　　我　家＿＿＿＿＿＿有　我　一
　　Wǒ　méiyǒu　xiōngdì jiěmèi.　　Wǒ jiā　　　　　　yǒu　wǒ　yí

　　个　　孩子。
　　ge　　háizi.

⑤ 你　家＿＿＿＿＿＿＿＿有　　什么　人?
　　Nǐ　jiā　　　　　　　　yǒu　　shénme rén?

Ⅲ. Grammar

Grammar Points

● The "有" sentences indicating possession

Subject + 有 + Numeral-quantifier compound + Noun

玛丽　　有　　一个　　妹妹。
Mǎlì　　yǒu　　yí ge　　mèimei.

金　太成　家　　有　　十 口　　人。
Jīn Tàichéng jiā　yǒu　　shí kǒu　rén.

● The sentence tag "了"

Subject + Numeral-quantifier compound + 了

赵　汉　　6 岁　　了。
Zhào Hàn　liù suì　le.

她 妹妹　今年　16 岁　了。
Tā mèimei　jīnnián　shíliù suì　le.

● The expression of "only have": 只有

Subject + 只有 (+Pronoun) + Numeral-quantifier compound + Noun

我　家　只　有　　我　　　一　个　　孩子。
Wǒ　jiā　zhǐ yǒu　　wǒ　　　yí　ge　　háizi.

他　只　有　　一　个　　中国　　朋友。
Tā　zhǐ yǒu　　yí　ge　　Zhōngguó péngyou.

● The construction "和……一起 / 一个人" as an adverbial

Subject　　+ 和……一起/一个人 + Verb

王杨　　　　和 父母 一起　住。
Wáng Yáng　hé fùmǔ yìqǐ　zhù.

我　　一　个　人　去。
Wǒ　yí　ge　rén　qù.

---

1 Rearrange the given words to form a sentence.

① 喜欢　　　住　　　人　　　我　　　一　个
xǐhuan　　zhù　　rén　　wǒ　　yí　ge

_____

② 只 有　　　词典　　　麦克　　　本　　　一
zhǐ yǒu　　cídiǎn　　Màikè　　běn　　yī

_____

③ 公司　　　有　　　名　　　职员　　　韩国　　　三　　　他们
gōngsī　　yǒu　　míng　　zhíyuán　Hánguó　sān　tāmen

_____

④ 80   外婆   玛丽   了   岁   的
bāshí wàipó Mǎlì le suì de

_____

⑤ 去   赵汉   一起   妈妈   上海   和
qù Zhào Hàn yìqǐ māma Shànghǎi hé

_____

2 Complete the following dialogues.

① A: _____ ?

B: 我 家 有 三 口 人。
   Wǒ jiā yǒu sān kǒu rén.

② A: 你 妹妹 今年 多 大 了?
   Nǐ mèimei jīnnián duō dà le?

B: _____。

③ A: 麦克 有 兄弟 姐妹 吗?
   Màikè yǒu xiōngdì jiěmèi ma?

B: 没有。 他 家_____。
   Méiyǒu. Tā jiā

④ A: 你 希望 和 父母 一起 住 吗?
   Nǐ xīwàng hé fùmǔ yìqǐ zhù ma?

B: _____。

⑤ A: 你 一个 人 去 上海 吗?
   Nǐ yí ge rén qù Shànghǎi ma?

B: 不,我 和_____。
   Bù, wǒ hé

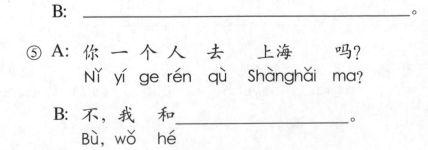

Ⅳ. Communication Skills

1 Fill in the blanks according to the pictures.

我 家_____ ：_____、_____、_____和_____。
Wǒ jiā   hé

爸爸_____。 妈妈_____。 哥哥_____。
Bàba   Māma   Gēge

我　现在　是　大学生，　我　希望_____。
Wǒ　xiànzài　shì　dàxuéshēng,　wǒ　xīwàng

2 Complete the following dialogues.

① A: 你 家 有 几 口 人?
　　 Nǐ jiā yǒu jǐ kǒu rén?

B: _____, 爸爸、 妈妈、 姐姐 和 我。
　　　　　　　　　　　　bàba、 māma、 jiějie hé wǒ.

A: 你 还 有 个 姐姐?_____?
　 Nǐ hái yǒu ge jiějie?

B: 她 今年 28 岁。 这 就 是 我 姐姐。
　 Tā jīnnián èrshíbā suì.　Zhè jiù shì wǒ jiějie.

A: 你 姐姐 真＿＿＿＿＿＿＿！ 她 在＿＿＿＿＿？
Nǐ jiějie zhēn Tā zài

B: 她 在 学校 工作。
Tā zài xuéxiào gōngzuò.

A: 你 希望＿＿＿＿＿＿＿？
Nǐ xīwàng

B: 我 想 当 律师，可是 我 妈妈 希望 我
Wǒ xiǎng dāng lùshī, kěshì wǒ māma xīwàng wǒ

去 银行 工作。
qù yínháng gōngzuò.

② A: 你 家＿＿＿＿＿＿＿？
Nǐ jiā

B: 爸爸、妈妈 和 我。
Bàba、māma hé wǒ.

A: 你 没有 兄弟 姐妹 吗？
Nǐ méiyǒu xiōngdì jiěmèi ma?

B: 对，我 家＿＿＿＿＿＿＿。
Duì, wǒ jiā

A: 你 一个人 住 吗？
Nǐ yí ge rén zhù ma?

B: 不，＿＿＿＿＿＿＿＿＿。
Bù,

A: ＿＿＿＿＿＿＿＿？

B: 我们 住 在 阳光 小区。看，那 就 是
Wǒmen zhù zài Yángguāng Xiǎoqū. Kàn, nà jiù shì

阳光 小区。
Yángguāng Xiǎoqū.

A: 啊，＿＿＿＿＿＿！
À

第八单元

V. Chinese Characters

Basic Knowledge

● Basic structure patterns of Chinese characters (1)

Structure pattern	Graphic illustration	Examples
Left-right structure	⊡	他 们 都 很 忙
Top-bottom structure	⊟	声 音 宿 舍 家

● Basic components of Chinese characters

钅 The radical 钅 (jīn zì páng), evolved from the character 金, appears on the left side of the characters with a left-right structure. The original meanings of the characters with 钅 as their radical are generally related to "metal". For example, 银 (yín), 钱 (qián), 铁 (tiě).

月 The radical 月 (ròuyuè páng) appears on the left side of the characters with a left-right structure. The original meanings of the characters with 月 as their radical are generally related to "body". For example, 胖 (pàng), 胞 (bāo), 胎 (tāi), 脸 (liǎn).

1 Determine the structure patterns of the following characters.

A——Left-right structure   B——Top-bottom structure

那（   ）语（   ）息（   ）休（   ）怎（   ）

家（   ）听（   ）字（   ）男（   ）时（   ）

汉（   ）要（   ）期（   ）星（   ）

2 Compose the following radicals into characters and form words with them.

① 钅 昔   （   ）_____

钅 艮   （   ）_____

② 月 半   （   ）_____

月 包   （   ）_____

月 台   （   ）_____

3 Practise writing the characters.

丿 二 千 禾 禾 禾 和 和

和	和	和								

丶 忄 忄 忙 忙

忙	忙	忙								

丶 丷 丷 屵 屵 尚 尚 常 常 常

| 常 | 常 | 常 | | | | | | | | | | |

丿 ㇏ ㇏ 钅 钅 钅 钉 钌 钖 银 银

| 银 | 银 | 银 | | | | | | | | | | |

丶 夕 彳 彳 行 行

| 行 | 行 | 行 | | | | | | | | | | |

一 二 丰 夫

| 夫 | 夫 | 夫 | | | | | | | | | | |

丶 冂 口 尸 兄

| 兄 | 兄 | 兄 | | | | | | | | | | |

丶 丷 丷 丷 当 肖 弟 弟

| 弟 | 弟 | 弟 | | | | | | | | | | |

丶 冂 口 尸 只

| 只 | 只 | 只 | | | | | | | | | | |

孩 了 子 子 子 孑 孩 孩 孩 孩

孩 孩 孩

呢 口 口 口 呼 呢 呢 呢

呢 呢 呢

双 フ 又 双 双

双 双 双

就 一 一 六 古 古 亨 京 京 京 就 就 就

就 就 就

送 一 一 一 一 关 关 关 送 送

送 送 送

父 一 一 分 父

父 父 父

母 乚 乜 乜 母 母

母 母 母

一 十 土 耂 耂 者 者 者 都 都

都	都	都										

一 十 廾 井 共 共

共	共	共										

Unit Nine

第九单元

我 最近 很 忙
Wǒ zuìjìn hěn máng

I've been very busy recently

Key Points

Subject	Time
Goals	Learn to ask and tell the time, and describe one's daily arrangements in simple terms
Grammar Points	• Point of time + "了" • Adverbials of time: Point of time + Verb phrase "……以前／以后" + Verb phrase • Questions with "几点" and "什么时候"

Focal Sentences	Major points in communication	Examples
	Asking and telling the time	现在几点？ ——现在 10 点 20。
	Telling what to do at a certain time	我每天 6 点起床。
	Polite forms to make inquiries	请问，现在几点？ 对不起，几点了？ 劳驾，第二医院在哪儿？
	Expressing uncertainty	不一定。

Words and Phrases	最近 点 半 劳驾 分 姑娘 差 愿意 能 时候 下班 行 到 吃 晚饭 开始 训练 先生 起床 以后 睡觉 这么 上班 加班 总公司 项 重要 不一定 有时候 星期五 有空儿 再说
Chinese Characters	点 半 劳 驾 分 姑 娘 差 愿 意 能 候 班 行 到 吃 饭 开 始 训 练 先 最 近 床 以 后 睡 觉 加 总 项 重 定 五 空 再
Phonetics	Syllable initials: zh ch Syllable finals: uan uang uen ueng Combination of tones

第九单元

Exercises

Ⅰ. Pronunciation

1 Read the following *Pinyin* aloud and pay attention to their different pronunciations.

zōng —— zhōng		zhèng —— zèng	
céng —— chéng		cōng —— chōng	
sì —— shì		sān —— shān	
sū —— shū		sǎng —— shǎng	
yuān —— yūn		yuán —— yún	
wàn —— yuàn		wèn —— yùn	

2 Read the following *Pinyin* aloud and pay attention to their different tones.

yīng	yíng	yǐng	yìng
yuān	yuán	yuǎn	yuàn
huā	hóng	liǔ	lù
bīng	qiáng	mǎ	zhuàng

3 Read the following words aloud.

劳驾　　姑娘　　愿意　　以后　　晚饭　　开始　　训练　　先生
láojià　gūniang　yuànyì　yǐhòu　wǎnfàn　kāishǐ　xùnliàn xiānsheng

最近　　起床　　睡觉　　上班　　下班　　加班　　一定　　当然
zuìjìn　qǐchuáng shuìjiào　shàngbān　xiàbān　jiābān　yídìng dāngrán

Ⅱ.Words and Expressions

1 Pick out the word that does not belong to the group.

① 最近   上班   下班   加班   (   )
zuìjìn   shàngbān   xiàbān   jiābān

② 新   一定   重要   漂亮   (   )
xīn   yídìng   zhòngyào   piàoliang

③ 开始   晚饭   起床   睡觉   (   )
kāishǐ   wǎnfàn   qǐchuáng   shuìjiào

④ 点   分   号   差   (   )
diǎn   fēn   hào   chà

⑤ 当然   愿意   要   能   (   )
dāngrán   yuànyì   yào   néng

2 Choose the right word to fill in the blank (1).

有空儿	有时候	不一定	以后	最近
yǒu kòngr	yǒushíhou	bù yídìng	yǐhòu	zuìjìn

① ＿＿＿＿＿＿＿金 太成   非常   忙，   常常   加班。
          Jīn Tàichéng fēicháng máng, chángcháng jiābān.

② 明天   我＿＿＿＿＿＿＿去。
Míngtiān wǒ   qù.

③ 菲雅   每天   晚上   12   点＿＿＿＿＿＿＿睡觉。
Fēiyǎ měi tiān wǎnshang shí'èr diǎn   shuìjiào.

④ 这个　星期六　上午　你＿＿＿＿＿＿＿＿＿吗?
Zhège　xīngqīliù　shàngwǔ　nǐ　　　　　　　　ma?

⑤ 李　冬生　　　早上＿＿＿＿＿＿＿7　点　起床,
Lǐ Dōngshēng　zǎoshang　　　　　　qī diǎn　qǐchuáng,

有时候　8　点　起床。
yǒushíhou　bā diǎn　qǐchuáng.

Choose the right word to fill in the blank (2).

> 下班　　愿意　　劳驾　　加班　　开始
> xiàbān　yuànyì　láojià　jiābān　kāishǐ

① ＿＿＿＿＿＿＿＿＿, 现在　几　点?
　　　　　　　　　　xiànzài　jǐ diǎn?

② 我们　下午　5　点　半＿＿＿＿＿＿＿训练。
Wǒmen xiàwǔ wǔ diǎn bàn　　　　　　xùnliàn.

③ 你＿＿＿＿＿＿＿当　我　的　健身　教练　吗?
Nǐ　　　　　　dāng wǒ de jiànshēn jiàoliàn ma?

④ 经理　要　我　星期六　去＿＿＿＿＿＿＿。
Jīnglǐ yào wǒ xīngqīliù qù

⑤ 她　下午　常常　　　6　点＿＿＿＿＿＿＿。
Tā xiàwǔ chángcháng　liù diǎn

Ⅲ. Grammar

Grammar Points

● Point of time + 了

10 点 50 分 了。
Shí diǎn wǔshí fēn le.

现在 8 点 半 了。
Xiànzài bā diǎn bàn le.

● Adverbials of time: Point of time + Verb phrase

"……以前／以后" + Verb phrase

Subject + Point of time + Verb/Verb phrase

我 每 天 6 点 起床。
Wǒ měi tiān liù diǎn qǐchuáng.

我 8 点 去 上课。
Wǒ bā diǎn qù shàng kè.

Subject + Point of time + 以前／以后 + Verb/Verb phrase

我 晚上 12 点 以后 睡觉。
Wǒ wǎnshang shí'èr diǎn yǐhòu shuìjiào

● Questions with "几点" and "什么时候"

Subject + 几点／什么时候 + Verb/Verb phrase

你　几　点　　上班?
Nǐ　jǐ diǎn　shàngbān?

你　什么　时候　去　健身?
Nǐ　shénme　shíhou　qù　jiànshēn?

1 Put the given word or phrase in the right place.

① 星期六　　没有　课, A 我　可以　　B　9点　　C　起床。
　Xīngqīliù　méiyǒu kè,　wǒ kěyǐ　　jiǔ diǎn　　qǐchuáng.

（以后）
yǐhòu

② A　明天　　我们　　B　开始　训练　C。　（8点半）
　míngtiān　wǒmen　　kāishǐ　xùnliàn　　bā diǎn bàn

③ A 我　有时候　B　去　图书馆　C。　（下午3点）
　wǒ　yǒushíhou　　qù　túshūguǎn　　xiàwǔ sān diǎn

④ A　你　B　每天　C　吃　晚饭?　（几点）
　　nǐ　　měi tiān　　chī wǎnfàn?　　jǐ diǎn

⑤ 9点　　可以, A　10　点　B　我　C　没有　　时间。
　Jiǔ diǎn　kěyǐ,　shí diǎn　　wǒ　　méiyǒu　shíjiān.

（以后）
yǐhòu

2 Complete the following dialogues，using "几点" or "什么时候" based on the timetable.

早上 6:50	起床
上午 8:00	上课
下午 5:30	吃晚饭
晚上 7:00	去健身
晚上 11:00	睡觉

① A: _____?

B: _____。

② A: _____?

B: _____。

③ A: _____?

B: _____。

④ A: _____?

B: _____。

⑤ A: _____?

　　B: _____。

---

3 Complete the following dialogues.

① A: 劳驾，_____?
　　　Láojià,

　　B: 现在　　7　点　　50　　分。
　　　Xiànzài　qī diǎn　wǔshí　fēn.

② A: _____?

　　B: 我　下午　3　点　以后　有　空儿。
　　　Wǒ　xiàwǔ sān diǎn　yǐhòu yǒu　kòngr.

③ A: 你　明天　下午 6 点　来　好　吗?
　　　Nǐ míngtiān xiàwǔ liù diǎn lái hǎo ma?

　　B: _____。

④ A: _____?

　　B: 我　每天　晚上　7　点　吃　晚饭。
　　　Wǒ měi tiān wǎnshang　qī diǎn chī wǎnfàn.

⑤ A: 这个　星期六　晚上　你　有 空儿　吗?
　　　Zhège　xīngqīliù wǎnshang　nǐ yǒu kòngr ma?

　　B: _____。

IV. Communication Skills

1 Match the pictures on the left to the corresponding sentences on the right.

①

②

③

④

⑤

A 对不起， 我 星期
　Duìbuqǐ， wǒ xīngqī-

　五 　晚上 　要
　wǔ 　wǎnshang 　yào

　加班。
　jiābān.

B 劳驾， 几 点 了?
　Láojià， jǐ diǎn le?

C 请 问， 赵 玉兰
　Qǐng wèn， Zhào Yùlán

　住 在 这儿 吗?
　zhù zài zhèr ma?

D 劳驾， 24 号 楼
　Láojià， èrshísì hào lóu

　在 哪儿?
　zài nǎr?

E 请 问， 您 是 哪
　Qǐng wèn， nín shì nǎ

　国 人?
　guó rén?

2 Complete the following dialogues.

① A: _____?

B: 哦，　现在　7　点　半。
Ò,　xiànzài qī　diǎn　bàn.

A: _____?

B: 我　　早上　　6 点　　起床。
Wǒ　zǎoshang　liù diǎn　qǐchuáng.

A: _____?

B: 我　　每天 7　点 去　　图书馆。
Wǒ　měi tiān qī　diǎn　qù　túshūguǎn.

A: _____?

B: 对，　我　最近　　非常　　忙。
Duì,　wǒ　zuìjìn　fēicháng　máng.

② A: 请　　问,　_____?
Qǐng　wèn,

B: 差　　10 分　　8 点　了。
Chà　shí fēn　bā diǎn　le.

A: _____?

B: 我　　早上　　6 点　半　　起床。
Wǒ　zǎoshang　liù diǎn　bàn　qǐchuáng.

A: _____?

B: 9　点　　上班。
Jiǔ　diǎn　shàngbān.

A: _____?

B: 不 一定， 有时候 5 点 下班， 有时候 6 点 下班。
Bù yídìng, yǒushíhou wǔ diǎn xiàbān, yǒushíhou liù diǎn xiàbān.

V. Chinese Characters

Basic Knowledge

● Basic components of Chinese characters

目　The radical 目 (mù zì páng), originally developed from the image of an eye. The original meanings of the characters with 目 as their radical are generally related to "eye" or looking. For example, 看 (kàn), 眼 (yǎn), 睛 (jīng), 睡 (shuì).

1 Compose the following radicals into characters and form words with them.

① 手　目　(　　　) _____

　 目　垂　(　　　) _____

② 女　也　(　　　) _____

　 女　马　(　　　) _____

　 女　生　(　　　) _____

女　乃　　（　　　）＿＿＿＿＿＿＿

女　且　　（　　　）＿＿＿＿＿＿＿

女　未　　（　　　）＿＿＿＿＿＿＿

女　古　　（　　　）＿＿＿＿＿＿＿

女　良　　（　　　）＿＿＿＿＿＿＿

2 Mark the following homophones with *Pinyin* and form words with them.

（　　　）是　＿＿＿＿＿＿＿　　　　（　　　）在　＿＿＿＿＿＿＿

　　　　　事　＿＿＿＿＿＿＿　　　　　　　　　再　＿＿＿＿＿＿＿

（　　　）名　＿＿＿＿＿＿＿　　　　（　　　）见　＿＿＿＿＿＿＿

　　　　　明　＿＿＿＿＿＿＿　　　　　　　　　健　＿＿＿＿＿＿＿

（　　　）电　＿＿＿＿＿＿＿　　　　（　　　）叫　＿＿＿＿＿＿＿

　　　　　店　＿＿＿＿＿＿＿　　　　　　　　　教　＿＿＿＿＿＿＿

（　　　）有　＿＿＿＿＿＿＿　　　　（　　　）记　＿＿＿＿＿＿＿

　　　　　友　＿＿＿＿＿＿＿　　　　　　　　　纪　＿＿＿＿＿＿＿

3 Practise writing the characters .

丨 卜 ⺊ 占 占 占 点 点 点

| 点 | 点 | 点 | | | | | | | | |

丶 丷 丷 兰 兰 半

| 半 | 半 | 半 | | | | | | | | |

丿 八 分 分

| 分 | 分 | 分 | | | | | | | | |

丶 丷 丷 兰 兰 羊 羊 美 差

| 差 | 差 | 差 | | | | | | | | |

一 厂 厂 厂 厂 原 原 原 原 原 原 愿 愿 愿

| 愿 | 愿 | 愿 | | | | | | | | |

丶 一 亠 亠 产 产 音 音 音 音 意 意 意

| 意 | 意 | 意 | | | | | | | | |

⺈ ⼛ 𠂉 ⺼ 育 自 自' 能 能 能

能	能	能

一 ⼯ ⼯ 云 至 至 到 到

到	到	到

丨 ⼝ ⼝ 口' 吖 吃

吃	吃	吃

一 二 于 开

开	开	开

㇛ 女 女 女' 女厶 始 始 始

始	始	始

丿 ⺧ 牛 生 步 先

先	先	先

丿 厂 斤 斤 '斤 䜣 近

近	近	近

ㄟ 厂 厂 后 后 后

后	后	后										

丶 丷 丷 丷 兯 兯 总 总 总

总	总	总										

丶 丷 宀 宀 宁 宇 定 定

定	定	定										

一 丁 万 五

五	五	五										

丶 丷 宀 宀 宍 空 空 空

空	空	空										

Unit Ten

第十单元

我来介绍一下儿
Wǒ lái jièshào yíxiàr

Let me introduce you

Key Points

Subject	Basic personal information
Goals	Learn to briefly introduce someone's basic information
Grammar Points	• Adverbial of time • Adverbial of place • Sentences with an adjectival predicate（"很／非常／真＋Adjective" or "太＋Adjective＋了"） • Verb＋"一下儿"／Reduplication of the verb

Focal Sentences	Major points in communication	Examples
	Asking if someone is free	你什么时候有时间？
	Telling what to do at a certain time	我们星期三下午三点半去健身。
	Introducing A and B to each other	我来介绍一下儿。这是麦克，我的健身教练。这是我姐姐张芳芳。
	Telling one's address	我住在 6 号楼 433 房间。

Words and Phrases	这 真的 没什么 欢迎 下次（下、次） 星期三 好的 朋友 女儿 学 教 时间 没有 课 给 打
Chinese Characters	真 迎 次 三 教 间 课 打
Phonetics	Syllable initials：sh r Syllable finals：uei üe üan ün Combination of tones

Exercises

Ⅰ. Pronunciation

1 Read the following *Pinyin* aloud and pay attention to their different pronunciations.

rè	—— lè	——	nè
róng	—— lóng	——	nóng
zī	—— zhī	——	jī
cī	—— chī	——	qī
sī	—— shī	——	xī

2 Read the following *Pinyin* aloud and pay attention to their different tones.

rēng	rú	rǔ	rè
(ēr)	ér	ěr	èr
shēn	móu	yuǎn	lù
shān	qióng	shuǐ	jìn

3 Read the following words aloud.

女儿	没有	时间	欢迎
nǚ'ér	méiyǒu	shíjiān	huānyíng

Ⅱ.Words and Expressions

1 Pick out the word that does not belong to the group.

① 爸爸　　妈妈　　女儿　　　学生　　　　　（　　　　）
　　bàba　　māma　　nǚ'ér　　xuésheng

② 学　　次　　教　　打　　　　　　　　　（　　　　）
　　xué　　cì　　jiāo　　dǎ

③ 欢迎　　　　介绍　　时间　　健身　　　　（　　　　）
　　huānyíng　　jièshào　shíjiān　jiànshēn

④ 印尼　　法语　　汉语　　日语　　　　　（　　　　）
　　Yìnní　　Fǎyǔ　　Hànyǔ　　Rìyǔ

⑤ 下午　　　晚上　　没有　　星期三　　　（　　　　）
　　xiàwǔ　　wǎnshang　méiyǒu　xīngqīsān

2 Choose the right word to fill in the blank.

欢迎	没有	教	学	打
huānyíng	méiyǒu	jiāo	xué	dǎ

① 对不起，　星期三　我_____时间。
　Duìbuqǐ,　xīngqīsān wǒ　　　　　shíjiān.

② 我　不　想_____法语。
　Wǒ　bù　xiǎng　　　　　　　　Fǎyǔ.

③ _____你们　来　我　家。
　　　　　　　　　　nǐmen　lái　wǒ　jiā.

④ 你　什么　　时候　给 我＿＿＿＿＿＿＿＿＿＿电话？
Nǐ　shénme　shíhou　gěi wǒ　　　　　　　　diànhuà?

⑤ 我　想　　学习　京剧，你＿＿＿＿＿＿＿＿＿＿我，好　吗？
Wǒ　xiǎng　xuéxí　jīngjù, nǐ　　　　　　　　wǒ, hǎo ma?

III. Grammar

Grammar Points

● Adverbial of time

Subject + Adverbial of time ＋ Verb/Verb phrase + Noun

我　　星期三　　晚上　　去 健身。
Wǒ　xīngqīsān wǎnshang　qù jiànshēn.

她　　明天　　学习　　京剧。
Tā　míngtiān　xuéxí　jīngjù.

● Adverbial of place

Subject + Adverbial of place + Verb ＋ Noun

玛丽　在 六 号 楼　　住。
Mǎlì　zài liù hào lóu　zhù.

我　在 家　等　你。
Wǒ　zài jiā　děng　nǐ.

● Sentences with an adjectival predicate

Subject ＋　很／非常／真 ＋ Adjective

他　　很　　　帅。
Tā　　hěn　　shuài.

你　　真　　　漂亮！
Nǐ　　zhēn　　piàoliang!

太　＋ Adjective ＋ 了

太　好　了！
Tài　hǎo　le!

这个　　医院　　太　远　了！
Zhège yīhuàn　tài　yuǎn　le!

● Verb＋ 一下儿 ／ Reduplication of the verb

Subject ＋Verb / Verb phrase ＋ 一下儿

我　　来　介绍　　　一下儿。
Wǒ　　lái　jièshào　　yíxiàr.

你　　试　　一下儿。
Nǐ　　shì　　yíxiàr.

Subject ＋ Reduplication of the verb ＋ Noun/Pronoun

你　　教教　　　我。
Nǐ　　jiāojiao　　wǒ.

我　　看看。
Wǒ　　kànkan.

1 Complete the sentences according to the pictures.

① 他＿＿＿＿＿＿＿＿＿＿高！
　Tā　　　　　　　gāo!

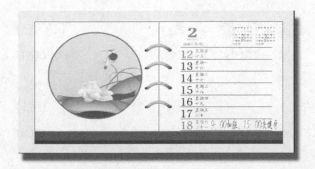

② 他＿＿＿＿＿＿＿＿＿＿加班。
　Tā　　　　　　　jiābān.

③ 我＿＿＿＿＿＿＿你的
　Wǒ　　　　　　nǐ de

　画儿，可以 吗?
　huàr, kěyǐ ma?

④ 我 来＿＿＿＿＿＿＿＿，
　Wǒ lái

　这 是 我 姐姐。
　zhè shì wǒ jiějie.

⑤ 我 在＿＿＿＿＿＿＿＿
　Wǒ zài

　等 你。
　děng nǐ.

2 Put the given word in the right place.

① 我　A　阳光　　小区　　B　住　C。　　　　　　　　　（在）
　　Wǒ　　Yángguāng Xiǎoqū　　zhù　　　　　　　　　zài

② 王　　杨 A 也　B 那 家 公司　　C　　工作。　　　　　（在）
　　Wáng Yáng　yě　　nà jiā gōngsī　　gōngzuò.　　　　　zài

③ A　　菲雅　B　　星期五　　C　　没有　　课。　　　　（下午）
　　　Fēiyǎ　　xīngqīwǔ　　méiyǒu kè.　　　　　xiàwǔ

④ A　　我们　B　每天　　上午　　C　　有 课。　　　　　（都）
　　　wǒmen　měi tiān　shàngwǔ　yǒu kè.　　　　　dōu

⑤ 我　　A　来　B　介绍 C，　这　是 我 的　法语 老师。
　　Wǒ　　lái　　jièshào　zhè　shì wǒ de　Fǎyǔ lǎoshī.

　　　　　　　　　　　　　　　　　　　　　　　　（一下儿）
　　　　　　　　　　　　　　　　　　　　　　　　yíxiàr

3 Complete the following dialogues.

① A：我 来_____，这 是 菲雅，我 的 学生。
　　　Wǒ lái　　　　　　　　　zhè shì Fēiyǎ, wǒ de xuésheng.

　　B：菲 雅，你 好!
　　　Fēiyǎ, nǐ hǎo!

② A：你 在　学校　　住 吗?
　　　Nǐ zài　xuéxiào　zhù ma?

　　B：对，我_____。
　　　Duì, wǒ

③ A：下 次 你_____去 健身?
　　　Xià cì nǐ　　　　　　　　　qù jiànshēn?

B：明天　　下午　两　　点。
　　Míngtiān　xiàwǔ liǎng diǎn.

④ A：_____?

B：金　太成　在一家　韩国　公司　工作。
　　Jīn Tàichéng　zài yì jiā Hánguó gōngsī gōngzuò.

⑤ A：您_____教　英语?
　　Nín　　　　　　　jiāo Yīngyǔ?

B：我　在　大学　教　英语。
　　Wǒ zài　dàxué jiāo Yīngyǔ.

A：哦，您是　英语　老师，_____, 好　吗?
　　Ò, nín shì Yīngyǔ lǎoshī,　　　　　　　　hǎo ma?

B：好　啊，我教你。
　　Hǎo a, wǒ jiāo nǐ.

IV. Communication Skills

1 Complete the following dialogues.

① A：_____?

B：我　星期三　有　时间。
　　Wǒ xīngqīsān yǒu shíjiān.

② A：你　明天　上午　还是　下午　有　空儿?
　　Nǐ míngtiān shàngwǔ háishi xiàwǔ yǒu kòngr?

B：_____。

③ A：_____，这是 玛丽， 英国 人。 这是
 zhè shì Mǎlì， Yīngguó rén. Zhè shì

山口 和子， 日本 人。_____。
Shānkǒu Hézǐ, Rìběn rén.

B：你们 好! 我 叫 王 杨。_____。
 Nǐmen hǎo! Wǒ jiào Wáng Yáng.

④ A：你 什么 时候 去 王 杨 家?
 Nǐ shénme shíhou qù Wáng Yáng jiā?

B：_____。

⑤ A：_____?

B：她 星期六 去 学 京剧。
 Tā xīngqīliù qù xué jīngjù.

2 Complete the following dialogues.

① A：菲雅，你 今天 下午 有 课 吗?
 Fēiyǎ, nǐ jīntiān xiàwǔ yǒu kè ma?

B：我_____。
 Wǒ

A：那 你 星期六 下午 有 时间 吗?
 Nà nǐ xīngqīliù xiàwǔ yǒu shíjiān ma?

B：_____。你 有 什么 事?
 Nǐ yǒu shénme shì?

A：我 想 和 你 一起 去 健身。
 Wǒ xiǎng hé nǐ yìqǐ qù jiànshēn.

B：哦，那_____吧。
 O, nà ba.

A: 好，　星期六　下午　见。
Hǎo,　xīngqīliù xiàwǔ jiàn.

② A: _____，这　是　我　朋友　菲雅。　这　是
zhè shì wǒ péngyou Fēiyǎ. Zhè shì

我　的　京剧　老师——赵　玉兰　老师。
wǒ de jīngjù lǎoshī —— Zhào Yùlán lǎoshī.

B: 赵　老师，您　好！我　也　很　喜欢　看　京剧。
Zhào lǎoshī, nín hǎo! Wǒ yě hěn xǐhuan kàn jīngjù.

C: 你　好！我　请　你们　看　京剧　吧。_____？
Nǐ hǎo! Wǒ qǐng nǐmen kàn jīngjù ba.

A: 太_____！我们　每天　晚上　都　有　时间。
Tài Wǒmen měi tiān wǎnshang dōu yǒu shíjiān.

C: _____？

B: 我　也　住　在　学校　的　宿舍。
Wǒ yě zhù zài xuéxiào de sùshè.

A: 那　我_____去　接　你们　吧。
Nà wǒ qù jiē nǐmen ba.

B: _____。

V. Chinese Characters

Basic Knowledge

● Basic components of Chinese characters

月　The radical 月 (ròuyuè páng). When it appears on the right side of the characters with a left-right structure, their meanings are generally related to "moon" or brightness. For example, 明 (míng), 期 (qī).

1　Compose the following radicals into characters and form words with them.

① 日　月　(　　　) ＿＿＿＿＿＿＿

其　月　(　　　) ＿＿＿＿＿＿＿

月　月　(　　　) ＿＿＿＿＿＿＿

② 相　心　(　　　) ＿＿＿＿＿＿＿

你　心　(　　　) ＿＿＿＿＿＿＿

乍　心　(　　　) ＿＿＿＿＿＿＿

自　心　(　　　) ＿＿＿＿＿＿＿

原　　心　　（　　）＿＿＿＿＿＿＿

音　　心　　（　　）＿＿＿＿＿＿＿

2 Find out the differences between the two characters in each pair.

大 —— 太　　　　大 —— 夫　　　　休 —— 体

儿 —— 几　　　　贝 —— 见　　　　只 —— 兄

刀 —— 力　　　　石 —— 右　　　　午 —— 牛

3 Practise writing the characters.

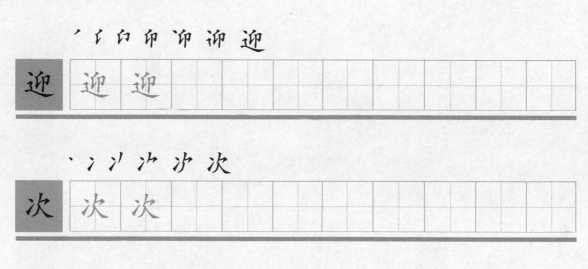

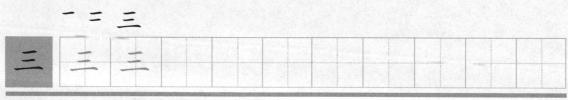

` 讠 订 识 识 识 课 课 课

课	课	课										

一 十 扌 扌 打

打	打	打										

Answer Key to Part of the Exercises

Unit One

Ⅱ.Words and Expressions

1. ① −D ② −C ③ −A ④ −B ⑤ −E

2. ① 你们 ② 是 ③ 谁 ④ 老师 ⑤ 您

3. ① 谁 ② 好 ③ 老师 ④ 是 ⑤ 你们

Ⅲ.Grammar

1. ① 你 ② 他 ③ 您 ④ 谁 ⑤ 是

2. ① 谁 ② 他 ③ 是 ④ 是、是 ⑤ 她是谁?

Ⅳ.Communication Skills

1. ① − B ② −E ③ −D ④ −A ⑤ −C

Unit Two

Ⅱ.Words and Expressions

1. ① 什么 ② 也 ③ 介绍 ④ 很 ⑤ 吗

2.(1) ① 姓 ② 也 ③ 叫 ④ 来 ⑤ 很

(2) ① 介绍 ② 叫 ③ 什么 ④ 高兴 ⑤ 学生

Ⅲ. Grammar

1.

① (×)请问,您贵姓?　　② (×)你叫什么名字?

③ (×)她认识李老师,我也认识李老师。

④ （×）玛丽也是学生。　　⑤ （×）他是老师吗？

2.

① 老师吗　　② 姓什么　　③ 叫什么名字

④ 我也很高兴　　⑤ 姓张

Ⅳ. Communication Skills

1. ① a　② b　③ a　④ b　⑤ a

Unit Three

Ⅱ. Words and Expressions

1. ① 护照　② 从　③ 谢谢　④ 但　⑤ 北京

2. (1) ① 从　② 哪　③ 吧　④ 再　⑤ 的

　　(2) ① 说　② 姓名　③ 给　④ 但　⑤ 地方

Ⅲ. Grammar

1.

① 他不是韩国人。　　② 她不姓张。

③ 他不是我的老师。　　④ 张圆圆不高兴。

⑤ 我也不认识李老师。

2.

① 你姓什么？　② 你是哪国人？　③ 你从哪儿来？

④ 玛丽是什么地方人？　⑤ 他是老师吧？

3.

① 哪国人　② 什么地方　③ 哪儿

④ 他是北京人　⑤ 美国人

Ⅳ. Communication Skills

1. ① － D   ② －C   ③ －E   ④ －B   ⑤ －A

Unit Four

Ⅱ. Words and Expressions

1. ① 公司   ② 工作   ③ 喜欢   ④ 在   ⑤ 大家

2.(1) ① 在   ② 画   ③ 名   ④ 做   ⑤ 家

   (2) ① 工作   ② 每天   ③ 哪儿   ④ 喜欢   ⑤ 现在

Ⅲ. Grammar

1. ① A   ② C   ③ B   ④ A   ⑤ C

2.

① 做什么工作   ② 在哪儿工作

③ 她在一家公司工作   ④ 这是我的护照

⑤ 对，我每天下午来图书馆

Ⅳ. Communication Skills

2. ① E   ②D   ③ A   ④ B   ⑤ C

Unit Five

Ⅱ. Words and Expressions

1. ① 几   ② 可以   ③ 事   ④ 几   ⑤ 好听

2.(1) ① 多   ② 几   ③ 年纪   ④ 岁

   (2) ① 猜   ② 事儿   ③ 好听   ④ 可以   ⑤ 真

Ⅲ. Grammar

1. ① A   ② B   ③ B   ④ B   ⑤ A

2.

① 赵汉今年几岁   ② 你猜他多大

③ 你爸爸今年多大年纪   ④ 可以   ⑤ 我看看

Ⅳ. Communication Skills

1.

① A：小朋友，你几岁？

    B：我四岁。

② A：你多大了？

    B：我 25 岁了。

③ A：大妈，您今年多大年纪了？

    B：72 了。

④ A：你认识李老师吗？

    B：我不认识。

⑤ A：我看看你的护照。

    B：给你。

Unit Six

Ⅱ. Words and Expressions

1. ① 找   ② 这样   ③ 不错   ④ 怎么样   ⑤ 漂亮

2.(1) ① 帅   ② 公斤   ③ 漂亮   ④ 累   ⑤ 米

  (2) ① 怎么样   ② 左右   ③ 这样   ④ 还是   ⑤ 休息

Ⅲ. Grammar

1.(1)

① 他的女朋友漂亮不漂亮? 　② 她高兴不高兴?

③ 你累不累? 　④ 他明天休息不休息?

⑤ 你看不看京剧?

(2)

① 你的教练是男的还是女的? 　② 明天你休息还是学习?

③ 金太成是经理还是职员? 　④ 你喜欢北京还是上海?

⑤ 你星期六上午来还是星期六下午来?

2.

① 他多高 　② 你多重 　③ 她很漂亮

④ 太帅了 　⑤ 他真胖

Ⅳ. Communication Skills

1.① D 　② B 　③ A 　④ E 　⑤ C

Unit Seven

Ⅱ. Words and Expressions

1.　① 饭店 　② 号 　③ 有 　④ 住 　⑤ 一会儿

2.(1) ① 当 　② 参加 　③ 接 　④ 住 　⑤ 有

(2) ① 饭店 　② 里 　③ 离 　④ 前边 　⑤ 晚上

Ⅲ. Grammar

1.　① B 　② B 　③ B 　④ C 　⑤ C

2.① 在 　② 离 　③ 从 　④ 在 　⑤ 在

Unit Eight

II. Words and Expressions

1. ① 姐妹　② 还有　③ 和　④ 忙　⑤ 银行
2. (1) ① A　② B　③ B　④ B　⑤ C
　　　　⑥ C　⑦ A
　　(2) ① 忙　② 送　③ 和　④ 只　⑤ 都

III. Grammar

1.

① 我喜欢一个人住。　　② 麦克只有一本词典。

③ 他们公司有三名韩国职员。　④ 玛丽的外婆80岁了。

⑤ 赵汉和妈妈一起去上海。

2.

① 你家有几口人　　② 我妹妹今年15岁了

③ 只有他一个孩子

④ 是的，我希望和父母一起住／不，我希望一个人住

⑤ 朋友一起去

IV. Communication Skills

1. 我家有四口人：爸爸、妈妈、哥哥和我。爸爸是公司经理。妈妈是大学老师。哥哥是大夫。我现在是大学生，我希望去银行工作。

Unit Nine

II. Words and Expressions

1. ① 最近　② 一定　③ 晚饭　④ 差　⑤ 当然
2. (1) ① 最近　② 不一定　③ 以后　④ 有空儿　⑤ 有时候

(2) ① 劳驾　② 开　　③ 愿意　　④ 加班　⑤ 下班

Ⅲ. Grammar

1. ① C　　② B　　③ B　　④ C　　⑤ B

3. ① 现在几点　　② 你几点以后有空儿　　③ 好的

④ 你每天晚上几点吃晚饭　　⑤ 我有空儿

Ⅳ. Communication Skills

1. ①－D　　②－E　　③－A　　④－C　　⑤－B

Unit Ten

Ⅱ. Words and Expressions

1. ① 学生　② 次　③ 时间　④ 印尼　⑤ 没有

2. ① 没有　② 学　③ 欢迎　④ 打　⑤ 教

Ⅲ. Grammar

1.

① 真　　　② 星期六上午　　③ 看看

④ 介绍一下儿　⑤ 长安饭店前面

2. ① A　② B　③ C　④ C　⑤ C

3.

① 介绍一下儿　② 在学校住　③ 什么时候

④ 金太成在哪儿工作?　⑤ 在哪儿　您教教我

Ⅳ. Communication Skills

1.

① 你什么时候有时间　② 我明天上午/下午有空儿

③ 我来介绍一下儿　认识你们很高兴

④ 我8点去　⑤ 玛丽什么时候去学京剧